The *Bewitched* ™
COOKBOOK

Magic in the Kitchen

The Bewitched™ COOKBOOK

BY
KASEY ROGERS
AND
MARK WOOD

KENSINGTON BOOKS

KENSINGTON BOOKS are published by

Kensington Publishing Corp.
850 Third Avenue
New York, NY 10022

First Kensington Printing: November, 1996
10   9   8   7   6   5   4   3   2   1

ISBN: 1-57566-095-4

Printed in the United States of America

In memory of Elizabeth Montgomery, whose Samantha has graced and enriched our television lives for more than thirty years; to Dick York and Dick Sargent for their wonderfully different portrayals of adman Darrin Stephens; to Agnes Moorehead, who single-handedly set the mother-in-law business back three centuries; to all the other monumental stars and guest stars who made *Bewitched* the icon of American television it has become today, and, finally, to all of you, the fans who've kept our characters alive for decades, we dedicate this book.

Best Witches,
Kasey "Louise Tate" Rogers

"We are quicksilver, a fleeting shadow, a distant sound.
Our homes have no boundaries beyond which we cannot pass.
We live in music, in a flash of color.
We live on the wind . . .

. . . and in the sparkle of a star."

Endora to Samantha, as written by Barbara Avedon.
[Episode #2, "BE IT EVER SO MORTGAGED"]

CONTENTS

Dining with the Tates, Louise and Larry 69

The Kravitz Kitchen—Gladys and Abner 93

The "Endorable" In-laws 117

Endora and Maurice 117

Phyllis and Frank Stephens 139

Serena's "I Hate to Cook" Quickies 149

Dr. Bombay's International Cuisine or 165
Around the World in 80 Decades with Dr. Bombay

FOREWORD BY SANDRA GOULD, A.K.A. "GLADYS KRAVITZ"

When I joined the cast of *Bewitched*, we became an instant family.

Since, next to acting and writing, I love to cook, I began to bring in goodies. Cookies, pies, a sixteen-pound pot of beef stew, a small ten-pound meat loaf (recipe on page 95). I quickly earned a reputation as "Mrs. Kravitz's Catering Service."

About that time, my home's orchard of 28 apricot trees became laden with fruit. To keep ahead of the birds who would peck one bite out of each apricot and then leave them all on the ground to rot, making the soil smell like a brewery, I bribed the cast with sumptuous Sunday barbeques to come over and help me pick the fruit. It was great fun, and they actually picked it. And picked it!

For weeks I put up jars of apricot jam, some with strawberries, pineapple, or tangerines, then gave them to cast, crew, and children's hospitals. I had labels printed reading "From the Unsanitary Kitchen of Mrs. Kravitz."

I was working my fingers to the bone. I even thought about asking Samantha to twitch her nose so the jam would magically be finished without my having to peel, split, and husk all that fruit. After all, as I was the nosy next-door neighbor, even if I saw her do it, no one would ever believe me. Mercifully, the apricot season came to an end before I did.

As I said, I do love to cook, but I hate too much fuss and work. Kasey and Mark have done a wonderful job of gathering traditional recipes from the cast, their families, and from friends of *Bewitched* and of simplifying most of them so the delicious results are easy to achieve. I hope you all enjoy *The* Bewitched *Cookbook* with relish. Or mustard. Or. . . .

Sandra Gould

"Gladys Kravitz"

INTRODUCTION

Bewitched
1964–1972

Does a sitcom about a comely young witch named Cassandra, her meddling mother, Matilda, and the young witch's new mortal husband, Darrin, sound familiar? Those were the original names of the characters in Sol Saks' pilot script for *Bewitched,* before the show found its star.

Enter Elizabeth Montgomery. For the next eight years, she would enchant the world as the now-renamed heroine, Samantha Stephens. Through the magic of reruns, *Bewitched* has been on the air for over 30 years! (Thank you, Nick at Nite and Ted Turner!)

Why a *Bewitched* cookbook? Well, why not? In the grand tradition of *Gilligan's Island, The Brady Bunch, The Andy Griffith Show,* and others, we couldn't leave *Bewitched* out. Besides, while a bona fide practicing witch can zap up a roast with the snap of her fingers, it seems a witch who marries a devout mortal must learn to cook by twitching her nose only to *smell* the roast. Samantha had to learn to cook from scratch the good, old-fashioned way, just like you and me.

Therefore, Mark and I have gathered together delicious, traditional family recipes, along with a few zingers from Samantha's witchly side of the family.

By combining these recipes with a collection of our favorite photos and some one-liners from *Bewitched,* we hope to conjure up heavenly memories and devilishly delicious dinners for you.

Kasey and Mark

Kitchen Tips

"The First Lady of Advertising"
Louise Tate!

OVEN

Be sure your oven is accurately calibrated. In many areas the gas company will calibrate your oven at no cost. If in doubt, buy an inexpensive oven thermometer. When cooking in glass utensils (such as Pyrex), lower oven heat by 25°F. to prevent over-browning or burning.

Remember that the center of the oven is the hottest location, and a cookie sheet that is too large will lower or affect oven temperature.

"I'm a Witch! A broom-riding, cauldron-stirring, house-haunting, card-carrying WITCH!"

—Samantha Stephens

MEAT AND POULTRY

Keep in the refrigerator or freezer separate from all other foods.

Let thaw in the refrigerator, *not* out on a counter.

After handling raw meat or poultry, throroughly wash working surfaces, cutting boards, utensils, and hands.

Cook thoroughly. Steak tartare and other raw meats, fish, or poultry are not safe to eat.

Keep hot foods hot. Immediately refrigerate any leftovers, or discard.

Put *that* in your cauldron and stir it!

MANY OF THE FOLLOWING FAVORITE RECIPES OF FAMILY AND FRIENDS ARE DECADES OLD. ORIGIN IS UNKNOWN.

Darrin: You'll have to learn to cook. And keep house. And go to my mother's house for dinner every Friday night.

Samantha: Darling, it sounds wonderful. And soon we'll be a normal, happy couple with no problems, just like everybody else. And then my mother can come and visit for a while and . . . oh . . . well, maybe we'd better work up to that gradually!

[Episode #1, "I, DARRIN, TAKE THIS WITCH, SAMANTHA"]

Dinner with the Stephens, Samantha and Darrin

Samantha Stephens

Contrary to what she told Darrin on their wedding night, Samantha was actually a Witch of great ability. Capable of destroying an entire dinner party with the wave of her hand, popping over to Paris on a whim, or revisiting the fourteenth century with a twitch of her nose, Samantha still chose to take care of her husband and children "in the everyday mortal manner."

Inheriting the powers of both her dynamic parents, the precocious child could fly before she was three and delighted in turning herself into a polka-dot unicorn or a postage stamp and traveling to Istanbul. "Those Turks are kinda rough," she once remarked.

Samantha was proficient in French, Italian and Spanish before Witchlet Kindergarten and could one-up Dr. Doolittle in "Animalese."

In the fall of 1963 Samantha met Darrin Stephens in the revolving door of Manhattan's Clark Building. Only a few hundred years old, (a teen-ager in Earthly years), Samantha did the unpardonable and fell in love with him, a mortal.

They married against the objections of her parents and the entire Witches Council, settled down in Westport, Connecticut and raised two children, Tabatha and Adam.

After a long and loving marriage, Samantha returned to the World of Witches to finish her reign as Queen.

On sabbatical, she visits her children, teaches her grandchildren the art of magic and awaits Darrin's reincarnation in the earthly sphere.

Samantha and her Darrins.
(Elizabeth Montgomery,
Dick York, and Dick Sargent)

COURTESY OF JOEY YORK

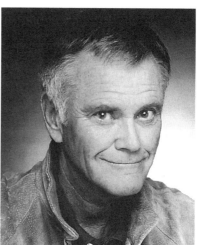

COURTESY OF DICK SARGENT

Darrin Stephens

"Once upon a time there was a typical American Boy . . ."

Darrin Stephens was about as typical as lips on a chicken! Let's face it, any *typical* mortal who married a witch like Samantha would have ruined his honeymoon by demanding she grant him the Midas touch!

Darrin was born in Morehouse, Missouri in 1933 to Frank and Phyllis Stephens. He was named for his grandfather, Frank Darrin Grover Stephens.

Darrin went to college at Missouri State, graduating *cum laude* in 1951. While there, he beat out his childhood friend, Dave, as student body president and could make the 100 yard dash in 10.3. Upon graduation he served in Korea under commanding officer Sargeant York.

Darrin joined McMann and Tate in 1961 and was made Account Executive in the spring of '62. That same year McMann and Tate moved their offices to the 32nd floor of the International Building in Manhattan.

On November 22, 1963, on his way to get his watch fixed, Darrin bumped into Samantha . . . and bumped into her! So he decided to ask her out before they had an accident! They shared a lovely, candlelit dinner at La Bella Dona and found they had a lot in common.

Not understanding why Darrin had suddenly become so distant, his fiancé Sheila left for Nassau to teach him a lesson. She came home to find that Darrin had married Samantha in a small civil ceremony on September 17, 1964.

Although vexed by a real witch of a mother-in-law, and an entire host of relatives he hadn't counted on, Darrin always said he wouldn't have traded his years with Samantha for anything in this, or any other, world.

Darrin Stephens departed this Earthly plane July 8th, 1994. He was 61 years old.

✳ Samantha's Mortal Menu ✳

Samantha: If you'll excuse me, I really have to get dinner started. I cook by mortal methods.
Ferdy: Oh really? Isn't that kinda messy?
Samantha: Yes, but it's more fun.

Samantha explains to Esmeralda's new fiancé Ferdy (Tom Bosley), the joys of "mortal-hood."

[Episode #226, "SAMANTHA'S MAGIC MIRROR"]

MENU

Samantha's Pot Roast with Vegetables

Carrots

New Potatoes

Small onions

Waldo's Warlock Waldorf Salad

Bewitched Be-Biscuits

Stroke of Midnight Chocolate Cake

with

Fluffy Cloud Nine Frosting

Louise: Is that pot roast I smell?
Endora: Hm-m-m . . . (She zaps a spell) . . . Smell again.
Louise: Well, that's not pot roast. What is it?
Endora: Lobster Thermidor!
Samantha: Mother, that wasn't necessary.
Endora: It is if *I'm* staying for dinner, darling!

[Episode #198, "Mona Sammy"]

Samantha's Pot Roast with Vegetables

On page 118 you will find Endora's version of Samantha's Mortal Dinner.

    4–5 lb. Pot roast (chuck, round, shoulder, or rump)
          Flour
          Salt
          Pepper

1   tsp. Sugar
½   c. Water
1   pkg. Onion soup mix

Have roast trimmed, rolled, and tied. Select heavy, deep pot with tight cover. Dredge roast with flour, salt, pepper, and sugar (for browning).

Grease pan lightly. Over high heat, brown roast well on all sides. (May take 30 minutes.) When dark brown, place rack under roast. Add ½ cup of water and package of onion soup mix. Cover tightly. Lower heat and cook very slowly for 2 hours.

Add:

Small whole potatoes
Tiny onions
Small carrots

Coat veggies with the onion soup mixture in the pot. Continue cooking for another hour or until roast is fork-tender. Don't forget to add a little more water as it cooks away, but never have more than 1 inch of liquid at any time.

Overall cooking time: 3 to 4 hours.
SERVES 8 TO 10.

"Double, double, Durwood's in trouble!"

[A publicity still from the pilot: September 17, 1964.]

Waldo's Warlock Waldorf Salad

Former beau, Waldo, once conjured up his very own Samantha (Episode #207, "Samantha's Bad Day in Salem"), which created a lot of friction between the "real thing" and Darrin. To make up for all the trouble he caused, he gave Sam the incantation for this enchanting salad. Here it is in mortal terms.

3	Green apples, Granny Smith or other tart apples
1	Red apple, Delicious or other sweet apple
1–2	Tbs. Lemon juice
1	c. Celery, sliced
½–1	c. Walnuts, coarsely chopped
½–1	c. Mayonnaise
2	tsp. Honey
	Iceberg lettuce, washed, dried, and crisped

Core crisp apples. Peel, if desired. (If peel is not tough it adds a nice touch of color.) Cube or slice apples into bowl. Toss with lemon juice to coat apples to prevent darkening. Add celery and walnuts. Cover and chill.

At serving time, mix mayonnaise and honey until smooth, add to apple mixture, toss, and serve on bed of lettuce.
SERVES 4 TO 5.

Bewitched Be-Biscuits

2	c. Flour, sifted and enriched
4	tsp. Baking powder
2	tsp. Sugar
½	tsp. Salt
½	tsp. Cream of tartar
½	c. Shortening
⅔	c. Milk

Sift together the flour, baking powder, sugar, salt, and cream of tartar.

Cut shortening in with pastry blender until mixture resembles coarse crumbs.

Add milk all at once and stir till dough follows fork around the bowl.

Dough should be soft and easy to handle. Turn it onto a lightly floured board, and knead gently a dozen times. Knead by folding dough and pressing down gently to blend ingredients and assure light, fluffy biscuits.

Roll dough out about ¾ inch thick. Cut with floured cutter and place on ungreased cookie sheet with a little space in between.

Brush with light cream before baking.

Bake at 450°F. for 10 to 12 minutes.

YIELDS 16.

Stroke of Midnight Chocolate Layer Cake

If the party was lovely and the gown divine, but your prince turned out to be a pumpkin, console yourself at the Witching Hour with my absolute favorite "blues" cure-all! This recipe dates back to the '40's.

1	c. Shortening
1¼	c. Sugar
1	Egg yolk
1	Egg, whole
1½	c. Flour, all-purpose
1	tsp. Baking soda
1	tsp. Baking powder
	Pinch Salt
1	tsp. Vanilla
½	c. Cocoa in 1 cup hot water

Cream shortening and sugar. Add egg yolk and whole egg. Beat. Add dry ingredients and vanilla. Last, stir in cocoa mixture.

Grease and lightly flour 2 baking tins (9 by 13 inches).

Bake in preheated (375°F.) oven for 30–40 minutes. When inserted toothpick comes out clean, it's done. Let cool in pans before turning out.

Wonderful topped with old-fashioned fluffy cloud nine frosting. (Recipe follows.)

Fluffy Cloud Nine Frosting

Combine in top of double boiler:

2	**Egg whites**
¾	**c. Sugar**
⅓	**c. Light corn syrup**
2	**Tbs. water**
¼	**tsp. Cream of tartar**
¼	**tsp. Salt**

Cook over rapidly boiling water, beating with rotary beater or electric mixer until mixture stands in peaks. Remove from heat.

Add:

1   tsp. Vanilla

Continue beating until thick enough to spread.

✳ Durwood's Favorite Client Dinner ✳

Samantha: O.K., but you tell Larry if I have to make one more dinner for a client, I want to go on the payroll!

[Sam to Darrin. Episode #200, "MAKE LOVE, NOT HATE"]

MENU

Parisienne Consommé à la Naomi

Darrin's Pork Loin Roast

Missouri-Style Horseradish

Minted Peas

Mother's Mashed Potatoes

Cold as Iceberg-Cucumber Salad

Nanny Elspeth's Perfect Salad Dressing

The Wicked Witch of the Yeast's Rolls

Cherries Jubilee Surprise

Parisienne Consommé à la Naomi

Naomi, the Stephens' first maid (Alice Ghostley's only non-Esmeralda role) concocted this tasty appetizer using Samantha's own recipe in Episode #53, "Maid to Order." Individual serving. Make for as many as you like by adapting recipe.

> 1   can Beef bouillon
>   **(Per bowl. Or 1 bouillon cube of any flavor.)**
> 4   slices Lemon
> 2   Tbs. Chives, minced
> 2   Tbs. Parsley, minced
> 1   oz. Sipping sherry, per bowl (optional)

Prepare beef bouillon (or cubes) as per directions.
Ladle into bowl. Float a slice of lemon in bowl.
Sprinkle with ½ tablespoon chives and ½ tablespoon parsley on broth.
Sherry may be added to hot bouillon or sipped on the side.

Samantha: I think I'll make him [Darrin] a pork loin.
Endora: Wouldn't it be more fun if you turned him into a whole
  pig?! Oink! Oink! Squeeeeal!

[Episode #126, "Snob in the Grass"]

Darrin's Pork Loin Roast

When done, meat thermometer should read 160°F.
A 3- to 4-pound roast will take up to 2 hours, a 5- to 7-pound
roast, 3 hours or more.
Allow a half pound of meat per person.
Ask butcher to bone, roll, and tie roast.

> **Roast**
> **Salt**
> **Pepper**
> **Herbs, such as thyme, oregano, or cumin; dry,**
>   **crumbled**

Basic Roasting Proceedure

Place roast on a rack, fat side up, in a shallow pan. Combine
salt, pepper, and herbs and rub lightly over roast. Insert meat
thermometer. Do not allow to touch fat.
When interior temperature reaches 160°F., remove from oven
and allow to rest for 15 minutes before carving.
Basic pork can be served with mint jelly, applesauce, or
horseradish.

Darrin: I'm from Missouri. Do you know what that means?
Samantha: What?
Darrin: Show me!

[Episode #1, "I, Darrin Take This Witch, Samantha"]

Missouri-Style Horseradish

Fresh horseradish roots
Salt
Sugar
Tarragon vinegar

Scrub and scrape fresh horseradish roots until clean. If you are doing a large amount, drop clean roots into water containing a couple of tablespoons of tarragon vinegar to prevent discoloring.

Drain and put through food processor or blender. Sprinkle liberally with salt and fill small jar ¾ full. Add a dash of sugar. Fill jar with tarragon vinegar and seal. Refrigerate.

"Lumpkin, pumpkin!
   Spider's eye,
If this mortal, he doth lie . . .
Whether told to friend or
   told to foe,
Each lie will cause his ears
   to grow!"

Endora casts another nasty!

[Episode #121, "My,
   What Big Ears You Have"]

"Ear's" to the Minted Peas

1–2   pkg. Small, frozen peas (Fresh shelled peas are even
        better.)
      Fresh mint leaves
1   tsp. Sugar
      Dash Salt
2–4   Tbs. Mint jelly

Place fresh or frozen peas in small amount of water. Bruise
fresh mint leaves. Add mint leaves, sugar, and salt to cooking
water.

Boil just until peas are done. Drain water. Add mint jelly, stir,
and serve.

Servings specified on packages.

Mother's Mashed Potatoes

"The secret of good mashed potatoes is *not* to use an electric
beater or food processor. Just wave your hands over the whole
potato and *voilà,* Instant Mashed Potatoes! Or have you mortals
invented those yet?

"Oh, all right! If you must drudge, you must . . .

"For light, fluffy, scrumptious mashed potatoes, use an old-
fashioned potato masher and mealy potatoes such as russets or
Idahos. Allow 1 small-to-medium potato per person."

[—Endora to Kasey]

6   medium Potatoes
¼   c. Butter
¾   c. Hot milk
      Salt, to taste
      Pepper, to taste, fresh ground

Peel and quarter potatoes. Place in large saucepan and cover with cold water. Boil gently until tender, 15 or 20 minutes. Drain well and reserve the liquid.

Add butter and small amount of milk. Begin mashing potatoes. Add milk as needed. When all the lumps are out, transfer to warm bowl and whisk until light, adding salt, pepper, and more milk, if necessary.

Good, light mashed potatoes are memorable.

Samantha: Darrin, I'm leaving you!
Darrin: Sam?
Samantha: I'm going home to mother.
Darrin: What do you mean "going home to mother?" Your mother's always here!

[Episode #96, "THREE WISHES"]

"It's for you!"

[A publicity still from the first season.]

Cold as Iceberg-Cucumber Salad

Iceberg lettuce, torn by hand or shredded
Cucumbers, sliced or cubed
Nanny Elspeth's Salad Dressing
Parmesan cheese, grated (optional)

Wash and dry lettuce well. Crisp in plastic bowls with airtight lids. May be stored for 2 or 3 days.

To serve:

Place desired amount of lettuce in salad bowl, add cucumbers, toss with salad dressing, sprinkle with Parmesan cheese, and serve iceberg-cold.

Nanny Elspeth's Salad Dressing

Her flying umbrella being in the shop, Nanny had to phone this one in.

⅔   **c. Extra virgin olive oil**
⅓   **c. Red wine vinegar (Try balsamic)**
3   **Tbs. Water**
3   **cloves Garlic, crushed**
1   **tsp. Sugar**
    Catsup to color
    Salt, to taste
    Pepper, to taste

Mix all ingredients and shake well. *Voilà!*

[Nanny Elspeth played by Hermione Baddeley

Episode #122, "I GET YOUR NANNY, YOU GET MY GOAT"]

Darrin: Your mother is worse than The Wicked Witch of the West!

Endora: Samantha! I refuse to stay here another minute and be compared to an amateur!

Wicked Witch of the Yeast's Rolls

1	Yeast packet
½	c. Sugar
1	tsp. Salt
2	c. Water, lukewarm
1	Egg, well beaten
7	c. Flour
3	Tbs. Shortening (Crisco), melted

Crumble yeast into bowl, add sugar, salt, water, and well-beaten egg. Mix vigorously until yeast is well distributed.

Sift flour before measuring. Add half of flour. Beat well.

Add melted shortening. Mix in rest of flour.

In a warm place (80–85°F.), let rise till dough doubles its bulk. About 2 or 3 hours. Do not disturb dough while rising.

If you are baking later, punch down, cover tightly, place in refrigerator, and *allow to rise again.*

To bake:

Punch down dough, cover, and let stand 10 to 15 minutes.

Butter fingers. Remove small pieces of dough and form into small balls.

Place 3 balls in each lightly buttered cup of a muffin tin.

Allow to rise again until nearly double in size. Maybe 30 minutes.

Bake at 350°F. until lightly browned.

YIELDS 36.

Darrin: Swell. I suppose you've got a great dessert planned.

Samantha: Um-hm. Cherries Jubilee.

Darrin: Boy. I should get that lucky.

Samantha holds out her hand, materializing a flaming Cherries Jubilee.

Samantha: You just have!

[Episode #53, "Maid to Order"]

Cherries Jubilee Surprise

This takes only a little longer than Sam's way.

1   **16-oz. can Cherries, dark, sweet, and pitted, undrained**
1   **Tbs. Cornstarch**
¼   **c. Brandy**
1   **qt. Vanilla ice cream**

Pour cherries and juice into a lovely chafing dish (or skillet). Dissolve cornstarch in a couple of tablespoons of cherry juice until smooth and add to cherries. Heat until liquid boils and thickens. Stir occasionally.

In separate pan, heat the brandy. Do not boil, just warm thoroughly.

While warming, scoop ice cream into individual serving dishes.

To serve:

Add warm brandy to the cherries and ignite.
Pour flaming cherries over ice cream and enjoy.
Spectacular!
(Caution: Any time you are working with flames, use extreme care.)
Note: Fresh Bing cherries may be used. First, pit them and cook in water (to cover) and a couple of spoonfuls of sugar. Proceed as above.

With her shopping out of the way Samantha is now ready to start Christmas Dinner.

✳ Samantha's Christmas Menu ✳

Christmas Twitch-or-Treat

Roast Turkey

Henry VIII's Herbed Sausage Dressing

Poppycock Turkey Stock

Aunt Hagatha's Gravy Potion

Santa's Ginger-Snappy Cranberry-Orange Mold

Aunt Clara's Fruit Cake

Durweed's All-Time-Favorite Lemon Meringue Pie

Samantha: Sweetheart, do you realize you are the only mortal
who can say he has actually met Santa Claus?

Darrin: Yeah! That's true! (Realizing) Who can I say it to?!

Christmas Twitch-or-Treats

1   c. Nuts (almonds, pecans, walnuts, Brazil nuts)
¼   c. Sugar
1   Tbs. Cinnamon
¼   tsp. Ground cloves
**¼   tsp. Nutmeg (Buy fresh nutmeg nuts and grate as you
    need.)**
1   large egg, Egg white only, slightly beaten

Mix sugar, cinnamon, cloves, and nutmeg together and put in
paper or plastic bag.

Put the egg white in a bowl, and beat it slightly. Dip the nuts,
a few at a time, into the egg white. Be sure they are coated thor-

oughly. Then, drop the nuts into the bag with dry seasonings and shake to coat nuts completely.

Place on a buttered cookie sheet and bake for 30 minutes at 300°F.

TURKEY ROASTING CHART

Based on U.S. Department of Agriculture Roasting Chart

Cooking times are approximate due to different body shapes of turkeys. Times are based on open-pan roasting starting with a chilled turkey in a 325°F. oven. Insert meat thermometer into center of thigh next to body but not touching bone. This is the last area to cook thoroughly. Thermometer should read 180°F. when done.

Weight (pounds)	Unstuffed (hours)	Stuffed (hours)
8 to 12	2¾ to 3	3 to 3½
12 to 14	3 to 3¾	3½ to 4
14 to 18	3¾ to 4¼	4 to 4¼
18 to 20	4¼ to 4½	4¼ to 4¾
20 to 24	4½ to 5	4¾ to 5¼

Allow one pound of turkey per serving.

Roast Turkey

Please read Meat and Poultry Tips, p. 2, before beginning.

Prepare turkey by thawing (if frozen) in refrigerator. This may take 2 or 3 days.

Remove neck, giblets, liver, and fat from turkey body. Wash and dry turkey inside and out. Salt and pepper inside and out.

Preheat oven to 425°F.

Pack the neck loosely with dressing (Recipe follows), fold skin over, and fasten with skewer. Pack the body cavity loosely and truss turkey.

Transfer remaining stuffing to a buttered 3-quart baking dish. Cover and return to refrigerator.

Spread on turkey ½ stick of butter. Insert meat thermometer. Place on rack in a roasting pan.

Roast at 425°F. for 30 minutes. Reduce temperature to 325°F. and baste with pan juices.

> 1 **c. White wine**
> 1 **stick Butter**

Melt butter. Cool and mix with white wine. Drape turkey with cheesecloth soaked in the wine and melted butter leaving meat thermometer uncovered.

Continue roasting, basting every 20 minutes for 2½ to 3 hours, or until meat thermometer reads 180°F. and juices run clear.

Remove from oven. Discard cheesecloth and string from turkey. Transfer to heated platter. Cover loosely with foil. Allow to stand 30 minutes before carving.

Henry the Eighth's Herbed Sausage Dressing

Samantha's Herbed Sausage Dressing is said to be the only dish that ever caused Henry to lose *his* head! If only poor Anne Boleyn had had the recipe!

> 12 **c. Day-old bread, Italian or French, cubed (two ½-pound loaves)**
> ¾ **lb. Bulk pork sausage**
> 1 **Tbs. Garlic, minced**
> 2 **c. Onion, finely chopped**
> 1½ **c. Celery, chopped**
> 3 **Tbs. Fresh thyme, minced (or 1 Tbs. dried)**
> 1 **Tbs. Fresh sage, minced (or 2 tsp. dried)**
> ⅔ **c. Parsley leaves, finely chopped**

1   stick Butter, unsalted, melted
    Salt, to taste
    Pepper, to taste
1   Egg, slightly beaten

In a shallow baking pan, arrange bread cubes in one layer. Bake in preheated oven, 325°F. for 10 to 15 minutes or until golden brown.

Transfer to large bowl.

In large skillet, brown sausage over moderately low heat, stirring until pink is gone. Transfer with slotted spoon to paper towels to drain. Pour off all but ¼ cup fat.

In fat remaining in skillet, sauté garlic, onion, celery, thyme, and sage, stirring until transparent. Transfer to the bowl. Add parsley, melted butter, salt and pepper to taste, sausage, and egg. Toss the stuffing well.

Allow to cool completely.

Stuffing may be made a day in advance, covered, and refrigerated. Do not stuff turkey until the last minute. Bake extra stuffing in covered casserole for 40 minutes.

COURTESY HERBIE J. PILATO COLLECTION

"Early one morning, just as the sun was rising,
I heard a maiden singing in the vale below:
'Oh! Don't deceive me, Oh! Never leave me . . .
How could you use a poor maiden so?' "

[Henry VIII (Ronald Long) looks on approvingly as Samantha sings for her supper in Episodes #229 and #230, "How Not to Lose Your Head to King Henry VIII"]

Dressing Reserved in Baking Dish

During the last 1½ hours of roasting turkey, drizzle reserved dressing with stock and bake, covered, at 325°F. for 1 hour. The last 30 minutes uncover to crisp up.

Samantha: Don't think of me as Mrs. Stephens, think of me as the Spirit of Christmas.
Mr. Mortimer: Poppycock!
Samantha: I had a feeling you'd say that.

Samantha deals with Scrooge-like client Mr. Mortimer (Charles Lane) in her own Christmas way.

[Episode #123, "HUMBUG NOT TO BE SPOKEN HERE"]

Poppycock Turkey Stock

(Do not use liver)

	Neck
	Giblets
5	c. Water
5	c. Chicken broth
1	rib Celery, chopped
1	Onion, quartered
1	Carrot, chopped
1	Bay leaf
½	tsp. Thyme
1	tsp. Peppercorns

In large stockpot, combine neck, giblets, veggies, water, and broth. Bring to a boil and skim off foam. Add spice and simmer on low for two hours or until reduced by half (5 to 6 cups).

Strain into bowl. Reserve the neck and giblets for gravy.

Stock can be made two days ahead and refrigerated.

Aunt Hagatha's Gravy Potion

For decades Enchantra has claimed this recipe to be hers, but the truth of the matter is it was tucked away in one of Hagatha's ancient volumes of potions. And it being the only one that was legible, we now offer it up for your approval.

1 **c. Dry white wine**
½ **c. All-purpose flour**
½ **c. Fat (reserved from pan)**
4 **c. Turkey stock**
    Neck meat (cleaned from bones)
    Giblets, minced
    Salt, to taste
    Pepper, to taste
    Parsley sprigs, for garnish
    Thyme sprigs, for garnish

 Could Samantha be trying to read up on how to cook Christmas dinner the mortal way?

[AN EARLY PUBLICITY STILL FROM *BEWITCHED*'S FIRST SEASON.]

Skim all fat from roasting pan. Reserve ½ cup fat.

Add 1 cup dry white wine to pan.

Deglaze pan over moderate heat scraping up brown bits. Boil mixture until reduced by ½.

In a saucepan, combine ½ cup flour with ½ cup of fat, making a roux.

Over moderate–low heat, whisk for three minutes. Important *all* lumps are removed.

Add 4 cups stock, a little at a time, stirring for about 10 minutes.

Add chopped giblets, salt, and pepper.

Pour drippings/wine from pan into the saucepan.

Simmer for a few minutes more then transfer to gravy boat.

Dick York was one of the nicest, kindest, most talented gentlemen I ever knew. During his last years on *Bewitched* he suffered terribly from back problems. Though the back of his set chair and that of the lounge in his dressing room were made of hard wood, I never heard Dick complain.

In later years, confined to his bed and compelled to use an oxygen tank, he labored on behalf of the homeless, generating food, clothing, and medicines.

The last time I talked with him was near Christmas time. He was so excited because he had just obtained over 100 mattresses for the less fortunate.

Joey York, Dick's wife, stood lovingly by him all those years. Today she still resides in the modest home they shared for many years after *Bewitched*'s last episode.

—K.R.

"What difference does it make what we look like on the outside, eh? It's what we feel on the inside that counts, isn't it? We all grow older and our eyes get weaker, but what we've seen with our hearts remains forever a thing of joy and beauty."

Santa (Cecil Kellaway),

[Episode #15, "A Vision of Sugar Plums"]

Santa's Ginger-Snappy Cranberry-Orange Mold

1	8-oz. box Orange Jell-O
1¼	c. Boiling water
1¼	c. Cold water
2	Tbs. Lemon juice, fresh
¼	tsp. Cinnamon, ground
⅛	tsp. Cloves, ground
12	oz. Cranberries, fresh
	Reserve a few whole berries for garnish
½	c. Sugar
1	Orange, diced
¼	c. Sugared ginger, chopped finely
½	c. Walnuts, chopped (optional)
	Orange and/or lemon slices for garnish
	Parsley for garnish

Dissolve Jell-O in boiling water. Add cold water, lemon juice, cinnamon, and cloves. Refrigerate.

Finely chop whole, fresh cranberries in blender or food processor. Blend in sugar.

When Jell-O mixture is slightly thickened, fold in cranberry mixture, orange sections, sugared ginger, and walnuts (if desired).

Spoon into mold. Refrigerate until firm, about 4 hours.

Unmold. Garnish with citrus slices and reserved cranberries, and tuck in a few sprigs of parsley.

SERVES 8 TO 10.

> "Stars, sun, wind and tide . . .
> In the heavens where you abide,
> Before your powers, we do bow
> Bring Santa's helpers here and now!"

Samantha conjures up some Christmas magic.

[Episode #184, "SANTA COMES TO VISIT AND STAYS AND STAYS"]

Samantha: Darrin, all my relatives are out of town for the holidays.
Darrin: Where, out of town?
Samantha: The fourteenth century! Far enough?

[Episode #213, "SISTERS AT HEART"]

Aunt Clara's Fruit Cake

Always thought of as being nuttier than one, Clara found this recipe for a fruit cake marking a page in one of her tattered, old Grimmoires.

1	stick Butter
1	c. Dark brown sugar, firmly packed
1	tsp. Lemon extract
2	Eggs
½	c. Molasses

2	c. Flour
½	tsp. Baking soda
1	tsp. Cinnamon
½	tsp. Allspice
½	tsp. Nutmeg
¼	tsp. Cloves
½	tsp. Salt
½	c. Milk
1½	c. Candied pineapple
1½	c. Candied cherries
1½	c. Pecans

Preheat oven, 325°F. Butter two loaf pans. (For super clean turn-out, you may also line pans with foil and butter the foil.)

Household Trivia:

What is Samantha and Darrin's address and who was the realtor?

1164 Morning Glory Circle, Westport, Connecticut 06880 and Hopkins Realty Co. 203-474-6925

Don't bother trying, the call "cannot be completed as dialed"!

Sam and Darrin's house got a real workout. Do you know what other TV couple lived there? Hint: They lived in Cocoa Beach, Florida.

That's it! Dr. Alfred Bellows and Amanda used both the exterior and the interior of Samantha's home as their own. Gee, I wonder who possesses the deed to it?

Turnabout's fair play: Larry and I got to reside in Jeannie and Tony's house in our one kitchen scene together, Episode #128, "Hippie, Hippie Hooray."

And early shots of Abner and Gladys' house were shot in Tony Nelson's living room, but that was before he moved into the neighborhood!

Cream butter and brown sugar until light in texture. Add lemon extract and eggs, and beat well. Add molasses and blend well.

In separate bowl, mix flour, baking soda, cinnamon, allspice, nutmeg, cloves, and salt.

Now beat flour mixture into the butter mixture. Add the milk and beat until smooth. Stir in the candied fruits and nuts, and mix well.

Bake 1 hour or 1¼. When toothpick comes out clean, turn onto racks to cool.

To store, wrap in cheesecloth. Saturate cloth with brandy, then wrap airtight in foil.

You may omit brandy and just wrap airtight in foil.

Durweed's All-Time-Favorite Lemon Meringue Pie

As found in Episode #111, "Double, Double, Toil and Trouble"

Crust

1½	c. All-purpose flour
1	Tbs. Sugar
	Dash Salt
½	c. Unsalted butter, cold, cut into small bits
2	Tbs. Vegetable shortening
3–4	Tbs. Ice water
¼	tsp. Vanilla

Combine all dry ingredients and cut in butter and shortening until mixture looks like coarse meal.

Add ice water and vanilla and toss until the liquid is absorbed. Add another spoonful only if necessary.

Form dough into a ball, wrap in plastic, and chill for half an hour.

On lightly floured board, roll dough out till round and ⅛ inch thick.

Fold in half and lift into 9-inch pie pan. Open out the crust and flute the edges with your fingers.

To bake, prick shell with a fork, line with wax paper, and then drop another pie pan into the shell. Place on a baking sheet on a lower rack in a 400°F. oven and bake for 15 minutes.

Remove the extra pie pan and paper and bake 10 minutes longer or until pale gold. Cool in the pan on a rack.

Filling

¾	c. Sugar
5	Tbs. Cornstarch
1–2	Tbs. Lemon zest (grated lemon peel)
½	c. Lemon juice
¼	tsp. Salt
3	Egg yolks (Reserve whites for meringue.)
1½	c. Milk, heated but not boiling
2	Tbs. Unsalted butter
½	tsp. Vanilla

Combine sugar, cornstarch, lemon peel, lemon juice, and salt in a stainless steel or enameled saucepan.

Add the yolks, one at a time, beating well after each one, then stir in the hot milk in a stream. Add the butter.

Stirring all the while, bring to a boil and simmer for 2 or 3 minutes, or until thickened.

Remove from heat, stir in the vanilla, and cool for about 5 minutes. Spoon mixture into the shell and let cool to room temperature.

Meringue

3	Egg whites, at room temperature
⅛	tsp. Salt
¾	c. Sugar
½	tsp. Vanilla
	Sifted confectioner's sugar

Beat the egg whites and salt until they form soft peaks. Add the sugar, a little at a time, and beat until stiff. Beat in the vanilla.

Completely cover your cool lemon pie with the meringue, sealing the edges. Meringue may be heaped in the center like the Matterhorn, or swirled decoratively.

Lightly sift confectioner's sugar over the top and bake at 350°F. for 15 minutes, or until top is pale gold.

Once finished and completely cooled you can either eat it or follow Darrin's example and throw it at your mother-in-law!

Darrin's Busy Bar

Samantha's "Fountain of Youth" Sangria Punch

"From the Fountain of Youth,
A drink I pour . . .
You're ten years younger,
Than you were before!"

[Episode #78, "ACCIDENTAL TWINS"]

½ c. Orange juice
½ c. Lime juice
½ c. Light rum
1 fifth Brandy
½ c. Sugar
1 small Orange (sliced thin, slices halved)
½ c. Maraschino cherries
1 stick Cinnamon

Blend liquids with sugar, stir till sugar dissolves.
Add fruit and cinnamon stick. Let stand 1 hour.
Remove cinnamon. Serve with ice in punch bowl or pitcher.
SERVINGS 12 TO 14.

Merlin's Martini

Uncle Arthur's namesake (King Arthur, you know) had his favorite wizard whip up this lively potion for his court. Arthur naturally stole it, but would sooner perish on a slope in the Himalayas than admit it! "Do remember," he says, "Martini's must be prepared delicately, never in a metal container and never with a metal spoon or it will bruise the potion!"

Per drink:

> 2½ oz. Gin
>   **Dash Dry vermouth**
> 1 **Green olive with pimiento**

First: Chill your crystal martini mixer by filling with ice. Swirl around until container is well chilled. Pour off excess ice water.

Next: Pour gin over ice.
Add a dash or two of vermouth.
Stir gently. Strain into chilled individual glasses. Add an olive and sip slowly.

Note: For a very dry martini, you may ingest the vermouth and simply blow across the gin in the martini mixer.

Samantha: Aren't you gonna offer me a drink, Darrin?
Darrin: A Zombie for the lady, please!

Charlie's Choice Zombie

Charlie, the bartender, concocted this for Darrin when he was having a fight with Samantha in Episode #148.

1 oz. Puerto Rican rum
½ oz. Grenadine
2 dashes Pernod or Herbsaint
1 tsp. Lemon juice
Seltzer

Stir first four ingredients with cracked ice and strain into goblet. Add crushed ice and seltzer to fill. Garnish with fruits in season and serve with straws.

Above dialogue and drinks featured in Episode #148, "Is It Magic, or Imagination?"

Darrin: What's the use of trying to fight a one-sided battle against Witchcraft? It's like trying to put out the Chicago fire with a bottle of pop!

[Episode #138, "The No-Harm Charm"]

Wily Wizard

A potent potion that any mortal can conjure up, guaranteed to drive away evil spirits, keep the werewolves at bay, and even make your mother-in-law seem more appealing. Works like a charm!

1 oz. Bailey's Irish Cream
1 oz. Amaretto
1 oz. Brandy
1 pint Vanilla ice cream
Maraschino cherry or sprig of mint for garnish

Put all ingredients in blender. Whir till creamy. Spoon into wide champagne goblets.

Garnish with a maraschino cherry or sprig of mint.

Note: Ingredients may be increased according to personal taste.

"Draft Beer, Not Students!"

Rarely did *Bewitched* reference current events, but this student's picket "sign of the times" said it all in the late '60's.

[Episode #87, "MY FRIEND BEN"]

Tituba's Toddie

For cold nights in front of a campfire or homey hearth. Serving for one.

1	big squirt Honey
½	Tbs. Lemon juice
2	oz. Rum
	Boiling water
	Nutmeg, freshly grated
	Sprinkle Cinnamon
½	slice Lemon

In bottom of heavy crystal or earthen mug, put generous spoonful of honey. Add lemon juice and rum. Fill with boiling water.

Grate nutmeg over, sprinkle with cinnamon, and float ½ lemon slice.

Dick Sargent performed probably the most difficult stunt ever on *Bewitched*; that of replacing Dick York as Darrin. He successfully helped keep the show running another three seasons. Here's to you, Dick.

Interestingly enough, Sargent was first considered for the role of Darrin in 1964. He was unable to accept the part due to his contract with Universal. Instead, he went on to star opposite Tammy

Grimes (Screen Gems' original thought for Samantha), in the ill-fated *Tammy Grimes Show.*

I've been asked many times which one was my favorite Darrin, and I've always answered truthfully, "The one named Dick"!

[—K.R.]

Trivia Strikes Again!

Darrin must have spent a lot of money on his first date with Sam. Two restaurants were mentioned as the location of their date! Can you name 'em?
La Bella Dona and Sorrento's

One of Darrin's "darring" Irish ancestors appeared twice in Bewitched. What was the wee fella's name?
Darrin, the Bold

In fifteen hundred and ninety-two, Darrin, the Bold, was supposed to "slew" who?
Rufus the Red (Played by Michael Ansara. Episode #79)

Another quickie! Who was Rufus the Red's girlfriend?
Hint: She was terribly afraid of cats and could weave a hole right out of a suit!
You got it! Jerry O'Toole the Wood Nymph (Played by Kathleen Nolan. Episode #79)

Darrin's Favorite
Breakfast Dishes

Darrin's Blueberry Pancakes

Bisquick
Butter
Blueberries or fruit of your choice (strawberries, bananas,
  peaches, or apples)
Syrup (My favorite is pure maple syrup, grade C.
  It's less refined.)

Prepare batter according to directions on box.
Melt butter on griddle.
Place 3 or 4 slices of fruit close together on hot griddle. Pour
batter over fruit forming perfect pancake. Flip when browned.
Stack. Serve with butter and syrup.

Sam's Super Strawberry Waffles

2	c. Flour
1	Tbs. Baking powder
½	tsp. Salt
3	Eggs, separated
1¼	c. Milk
¼	c. Butter, melted
3	Tbs. Sugar
¾	c. Frozen strawberries, thawed

In a bowl, mix the flour, baking powder, and salt.

In another bowl, beat the egg yolks well, and add the milk and butter.

Combine the yolk and flour mixture, and beat until smooth.

In yet another bowl, beat the egg whites until stiff but not dry. Add the sugar, little by little, as you continue beating.

Take ⅓ of the beaten egg whites and the frozen strawberries, and gently mix them into the batter. Now gently fold in the remaining egg white.

Pour about ½ cup of waffle batter onto the hot, greased (if necessary) waffle iron.

Bake until golden brown. Spoon additional thawed strawberries on top of waffles.

YIELDS 11 WAFFLES.

Darrin: You gave me those three wishes to make a fool out of me, didn't you?

Endora: Wel-l-l-l-l . . .

Darrin: I can make a fool out of myself without any help from you!

[Episode #96, "THREE WISHES"]

Endora's Eggs Benedict Arnold

Recipe is for one person. Multiply as needed.

1	**English muffin, split and toasted**
	Butter
2–4	**slices Canadian bacon**
2	**Eggs, poached**
	Hollandaise sauce (Make ahead; recipe follows.)
	Sliced fresh fruit for garnish (optional)

Split English muffin, butter both sides, and toast.
Fry Canadian bacon lightly.
Poach eggs by gently slipping each egg from a saucer or cup into simmering water. Simmer 3 to 5 minutes until white is firm and yolk still runny. Remove with slotted spoon to drain water.
To assemble, place toasted English muffin halves on plate.
Cover each side with 1 or 2 slices of hot Canadian bacon.
Top each with poached egg and a couple of dollops of hollandaise sauce.
Garnish with slices of fresh fruit.

Hagatha's Hollandaise Sauce

Another classic.

3	**Egg yolks**
2 or 3	**Tbs. Fresh lemon juice**
1	**cube Butter, melted**
2	**Tbs. Hot water**
	Salt, to taste
	Cayenne (optional)

Place water in bottom of double boiler and heat until hot, *not* simmering or boiling, just hot.

Place the egg yolks in top of double boiler and beat with wire whisk until smooth. Not too much. Not fluffy, just smooth.

Continue beating as, one at a time, you add the lemon juice, butter, hot water, salt, and cayenne (optional).

Beat for about 5 minutes, until the sauce is fairly thick. It will thicken more as it cools. Makes about ¾ cup.

Serve immediately or warm over heated water for up to two hours.

Great over steamed, green vegetables, with fish, chicken, and Eggs Benedict.

If your hollandaise curdles a bit, which Darrin claimed Endora could make happen at a glance, whisk in a very few drops of hot water to smooth it out. Add a few more, if necessary. If you want to cheat, the market does carry hollandaise in cans, but freshly made is always better.

Left to right: Dick York, William Asher, Elizabeth Montgomery, and producer Harry Ackerman celebrate *Bewitched*'s fifth season. September of '68.

The Bewitched Fifth Season Celebration Cake

1	6-oz. can Frozen lemonade
¾	c. Sugar
1	3-oz. box Lemon Jell-O
¾	c. Hot water
4	Eggs
½	c. Cooking oil (Mazola)
1	box Duncan Hines White Cake Mix

Thaw frozen lemonade and dissolve ¾ cup of sugar in it and set aside. Stir occasionally.

Mix lemon Jell-O with ¾ cup of hot water. Set aside to cool.

Beat eggs and oil together, then add cake mix. Fold in lemon Jell-O.

Pour into greased tube pan. Bake at 325°F. for 1 hour. Remove from oven and loosen sides before spooning lemonade mixture over cake. Cool cake in pan allowing lemonade mixture to soak in. Turn upside down on wax paper to remove.

Tabatha and Adam

Tabatha (Original spelling) and Adam

The biggest question in television history was "Is she or isn't she?" Referring, of course, to Tabatha's ability to cast magic spells. The answer, a resounding "YES", was revealed in BEWITCHED'S first color episode on September 15, 1966, just twenty-one episodes after she was born (January 13, 1966). Darrin was finally told a week later as Larry and Louise helped them celebrate their anniversary.

Tabatha's antics as a child kept the Stephens household in a continuous uproar. After all, trying to explain away a real live Mother Goose, Artful Dodger or Prince Charming to her mortal grandparents and teachers would be enough to give anyone a sick headache!

Tabatha eventually moved to Los Angeles and landed a job as a Production Assistant at KXLA. Today, she has given up her career to be a wife and mother of three. Tabatha now resides in Delaware.

✳ "Darrin . . . you're going to be a dad!"

Adam

Adam Frank Maurice Stephens was born on October 10, 1969 (Episode #175 "And Something Makes Four"). As a child, Adam, was never sure which side of the Mortal/Witch coin he landed on. However, in the ninth grade he finally developed "Wish-craft" much to the chagrin of his father and the elation of his "Heretical" grandparents.

Preferring the "Straight and Mortal" way of life, Adam decided to follow in his father's footsteps (much to the elation of his father and the chagrin of his heretical grandparents!) and became an account executive at McMann and Tate.

Today, Adam still resides in Manhattan, is married, and toils daily as an account executive at McMann, Tate and Stephens.

Fun recipes Little Kitchen Witches and Warlocks can make with help from the Main Kitchen Witch.

✳ Tabatha's Tea Party ✳

MENU
Tabatha's Tiny Tea

Adam's Apple Sparkler Punch

Sticky Finger Sandwitches

Chickie Sandwitches #1 & #2

Oh, My Stars! Cookies

A Giant's Happy Hermits

Darrin: Not Endora? Not Aunt Clara? Wh-who else, then? It's not . . . uh . . . not . . . uhmmm "What's-her-name"?! She's just a baby! It's not possible!

Samantha: Darrin, you always knew it was *possible!*

Darrin finds out about Tabatha's imminent witch-hood.

[Episode #76, "The Moment of Truth"]

Tabatha's Tiny Tea

Apple, Raspberry, Camomile or . . .

Be sure any "tea" brewed for children is *decaffeinated* and made from healthy fruit and herbs.

Brew a tiny pot according to directions. Add a bit more water if you wish to dilute.

Add a splash of milk and sweeten with a touch of honey.

Adam's Apple Sparkler Punch

1   **gal. Apple cider (or apple juice)**
2   **2-liter Sprites (caffeine free O.K.)**

Pour over Gigantic Ice Cube. (See Louise Tate chapter.) That's it!.

Great for kids parties and adults love it.

Sticky Finger Sandwitches

1   **loaf Whole wheat bread**
     Bananas
     Peanut butter
     Honey

The Main Kitchen Witch will trim crusts from the bread and slice the bananas. Little Kitchen Witches may spread the peanut butter lightly on two slices of bread. On one slice, cover peanut butter with slices of banana and drizzle honey over all. Place the second slice on top, peanut butter inside. Slice from corner to corner.

Chickie Sandwitch #1

1   3¼-oz. can White chicken
½   c. Mayonnaise
¼   c. Celery, chopped
¼   c. Green or seedless red grapes, split
    Lettuce (optional)
2   slices Bread

Drain chicken. Break up into small pieces and mix with mayonnaise, celery, and grapes until smooth. Add more mayonnaise if dry.

To assemble, spread mayonnaise on bread, if desired. Spread Chickie Salad on one slice. Top with lettuce.

Chickie Sandwitch #2

1   3¼-oz. can All white chicken
    Delicious apples (chopped)
    Raisins
    Mayonnaise
    Lettuce (optional)
    Bread

Drain chicken and flake into bowl. Add apples and raisins. Mix with mayonnaise until smooth. Place lettuce leaf on slice of bread. Cover with Chickie Mix and top with another slice of bread.

Oh, My Stars! Cookies

(Shortcut Version)

> 1   pkg. Sugar cookie mix (Buy at market.)
>   Star Dust (sugar)
>   Moon Dust (powdered sugar)

Prepare as directed. Use cookie cutters to cut dough into stars and crescent moons. Sprinkle stars with Star Dust (sugar) and sprinkle crescent moons with Moon Dust (powdered sugar).
Bake as directed.

Darrin: We have a beautiful, wonderful daughter, and I hope she grows up to be just like you!
Samantha: Something tells me you're gonna get your wish!

Samantha knows something Darrin doesn't, that Tabatha is a witch!

[Episode #75, "Nobody's Perfect"]

Giant: Now listen, little girl, I am about to lose my temper!
Tabatha: If you lose your temper, I'll make a "no-no" at you!

Tabatha threatens Giant (Ronald Long) with mayhem shortly before shrinking him to the size of a bug!

[Episode #171, "Samantha and the Beanstalk"]

A Giant's Happy Hermits

> ¾   c. Vegetable shortening (soft)
> 1½ c. Dark brown sugar, firmly packed
> 2   large Eggs, well beaten
> ⅓   c. Coffee, strong
> 3   c. All-purpose flour, sifted

1 tsp. Baking soda
½ tsp. Salt
1 tsp. Nutmeg, ground
1 tsp. Cinnamon, ground
2 c. Raisins, seedless
1 c. Walnuts, coarsely broken

Cream shortening until light and fluffy. Gradually beat in sugar; stir in eggs and coffee. Sift flour with baking soda, salt, and spices. Toss with raisins and walnuts. Add to batter, stir until well blended.

Drop mixture by teaspoons on a lightly greased cookie sheet. Preheat oven to 400°F. and bake for 10 to 12 minutes, or until golden brown. Remove with spatula, cool on rack. May be stored in airtight container.

YIELDS 36.

✳   ✳   ✳

What's in a Name? In Episode #54, "And Then There Were Three," Samantha gave birth to a baby girl that she and Darrin named "Tabatha." Erin Murphy once told me that her real father couldn't understand why they spelled "Tabatha" with all *a*'s, when the name should be spelled with an *i*, as in "Tabitha." Seems everyone agreed with him and by "Tabatha's" fourth season she was rechristened "Tabitha" in the credits. The 1977 series "Tabitha," Lisa Hartman, also used the *i* spelling. Kasey and I decided to use the original spelling to give it equal time!

✳   ✳   ✳

✳ Tabatha's "Exquisite, Brilliant, Charming, Perfect, Little Witchlet" Birthday Party ✳

MENU
Samantha's Indian Corn Necklaces

Baking Powder Biscuit Sandwitches

Blue Corn Chips

Icky, Yucky, Bloodshot, Scary Eyes

Incredible, Edible Chocolate Bowl of Ice Cream

Giant Peanut Butter Logs

Louise: A party? Why, isn't that sweet! But I don't want you to go to any trouble, Sam.

Darrin: Oh, no trouble at all!

Samantha: Oh, no. No, Louise, no trouble! Why, I can have every-thing ready just like that! *(Snap!)*

Samantha whips up an instant party on the back porch for Jonathan Tate's birthday.

[Episode #78, "ACCIDENTAL TWINS"]

Samantha's Indian Corn Necklaces

At harvest time, brightly colored Indian corn becomes available at roadside stands and sometimes in your supermarket. The dried kernels can be picked off, starting at the small tip and working toward the leafy end.

When all kernels are removed, cover them with water, and simmer 30 to 45 minutes or until soft enough to poke a needle through. Not so soft, however, that the skins split.

Now, string the kernels and hang them up to dry. The kernels will become hard again by the next day.

Wonderful for necklaces, garlands, or decorations.

For a more edible necklace, Mark strung candy corn last Halloween, using a blunt needle and thread. He ended up eating it all—with a little help from his friend. Me.

[—K.R.]

Baking Powder Biscuit Sandwitches

(Shortcut Version)

> 1   pkg. Baking powder biscuit mix

Bake according to directions. Split, butter, and fill "with your imagination."

1   Jelly or jam
2   Cheese
3   Tuna or chickie sandwich
4   Deviled ham spread
5   Cream cheese with honey and grated orange rind
6   Slice of ham with mustard
7   Just yummy honey

> "Close your fingers and cross your eyes
> Get ready for a big surprise . . .
> The rain is dry, the night is sunny . . .
> Hold and below, a cottontail bunny!"

At Tabatha's birthday party, Uncle Arthur pulls a rabbit from his hat, a sexy "Bunny" played by actress Carol Wayne. Darrin, Larry, and client Mr. Sylvester (Bernie Kopell) are thrilled.

Darrin: Pretty good trick.
Mr. Sylvester: One of the cutest tricks I ever saw!

[Episode #178, "A Bunny for Tabatha"]

Blue Corn Tortilla Chips

Buy a bag at most any good market.

"Darrin, don't worry, any baby that can be potty-trained can be Witchcraft-trained!"

Samantha to Darrin, after he worries about how to raise a baby witchlet.

[Episode #76, "THE MOMENT OF TRUTH"]

Icky, Yucky, Bloodshot, Scary Eyes

Kids are only grossed out over the things that are good for them, never by icky-yucky-gooey kinda things. This is a great way to get obstinate kids to eat "good for them" treats.

Tabatha agrees, they're perfect for Halloween.

6	large Eggs
	Mayonnaise
	Mustard
	Salt, to taste
	Pepper, to taste
Few	Black olives and/or Green olives with pimiento centers
1	tube Red decorating gel

Place eggs in large pot of cold water. Bring to a moderate boil, and cook for 10 minutes. Pour off water and allow eggs to cool completely.

When they are cool, shell, slice lengthwise, and scoop out yolks. To yolks, add mayonnaise, mustard, salt, and pepper. Mash and mix until smooth. Refill whites of eggs.

Place eggs, yolk *down*, on serving plate. Slice olives and place one slice in center of each egg for pupils.

With red gel, draw wavy lines on white of eggs, creating Bloodshot Scary Eyes.

"O.K., kiddies, here comes Uncle Arthur . . . Stuff yourselves!"

Uncle Arthur prepares to serve ice cream at Tabatha's Birthday party.

[Episode #178, "A Bunny for Tabatha"]

Incredible, Edible Chocolate Bowl of Ice Cream

Dipping chocolate (available at cake specialty stores)
Ice cream

In top of double boiler, melt special dipping chocolate.
Blow up a balloon and grease it.
Remove chocolate from heat and cool slightly.
Dip balloon in the chocolate halfway up. Be sure to dip until chocolate is fairly thick. Set chocolate balloon on plate forming a flat base for a bowl. Place in refrigerator to harden.
To serve, pop balloon and—*voilà*—an instant, edible chocolate bowl.
Fill with scoops of ice cream.
For Halloween, use chocolate and orange sherbet.
For birthdays, use many different flavors or choose a color scheme. Insert a birthday candle into each ball of ice cream and light for a festive birthday "cake."

Darrin: My daughter's a Witch! Samantha, I've got to know, how much of a Witch is she?
Samantha: Well, she doesn't really know what she's doing. It's all sort of involuntary. She wants something and she gets it!

Darrin resigns himself to the idea that Tabatha is a witch.

[Episode #76, "The Moment of Truth"]

Giant: That rascal Jack will be here any minute.
Tabatha: No, he won't. He's living in my house!
Giant: Nonsense, he comes into the castle on the next page.

Jack's Giant (Ronald Long) tries to reason with Tabatha to get her out of *his* story!

[Episode #171, "Samantha and the Beanstalk"]

Giant Peanut Butter Logs

Tabatha always insisted on making these for her (and Adam's) birthday.

Good and good for you. Yields 1 pound of high-protein candy.

First, wash your hands, put on a big apron, get a big bowl and big spoon.

Mix:

1   cup of natural crunchy peanut butter (nothing added)
4   Tbs. honey
1   tsp. vanilla

It will be gooey, but don't stop now.

Add:

Pinch of salt
1½   c. powdered skim milk

Keep stirring. You may need a dull table knife to help. When well blended, add:

Moon Dust (powdered sugar)

until it tastes not too sweet but just right!

Now, with your clean hands, roll into logs. Ask the Main Kitchen Witch to help you chop some peanuts. Then, roll the logs in the peanuts. Chill and slice if logs are large enough. *Yum!*

Samantha: Babies are such a nice way to start people!

Samantha to new son Adam as she cuddles him under the Christmas tree.

[Episode #184, "SANTA COMES TO VISIT AND STAYS AND STAYS"]

✳ Adam's Toddler Snacks ✳

ADAM'S BREAKFAST SNACKS

It's A Yolk, Son

Bread	**1 slice per person**
	Butter or margarine
Eggs	**1 egg per person**
	Salt
Syrup	**Any kind. (optional)**

With cookie cutter or knife, cut 2-inch circle out of center of slice of bread. Melt pat of butter (or margarine) in skillet. When hot, place slice of bread in the butter and break egg into center hole. Sprinkle with a little salt. When browned on one side, slide wide spatula under toast and flip it over. Continue cooking until bread is toasted and egg white done. Yolk should be runny.

Enjoy as is or pour syrup over for a faux French toast.

"He kept saying, 'There's no Santa, there's no Santa, there's no Santa.' So I turned him into a mushroom, and he finally admitted he was wrong!"

Tabatha telling her mother how she cured Sydney Kravitz of *not* believing in Santa.

[Episode #184, "SANTA COMES TO VISIT AND STAYS AND STAYS"]

Sydney's Home-Ground Quick Biscuits

This is especially fun if you buy whole grains from the health-food store and let the Little Kitchen Witches grind their own grain. Wee Warlocks love to grind whole wheat berries, oat groats, rye berries, even dried corn picked off the cob.

A hand-operated coffee grinder works well, or an electric grinder or food processor. Any mixture the Little Witches grind may be used for these biscuits.

> 2 **c. Flour (all one grain or a combination of grains)**
> ½ **c. Sucanat (or ¼ c. sugar)**
> ½ **tsp. Salt**
> 2 **tsp. Baking soda**
> ½ **cube Butter, melted**
> ⅔ **c. Milk (May be soy, rice, or dairy.)**
> **Jam (your favorite)**

Preheat oven to 450°F.

Stir all dry ingredients together. Stir in butter, then milk.

On lightly floured board, knead gently 5 to 10 times. Do not overwork or biscuits will be tough.

Roll into 1½-inch balls. Place on ungreased cookie sheet. Ask the Little Kitchen Witches to make an indentation in the middle of each ball of dough with their thumbs. (This little well will hold the jam.)

Bake 10 minutes.

Remove from oven and top with ½ teaspoon jam or Honey Butter.

YIELDS ABOUT 16 BISCUITS.

Honey Butter

Simple. Mix equal parts soft butter and honey.

Tabatha Trivia

Children are most always played by twins on TV shows. How many sets of twins played Tabatha?

Three. Infants, secondary, and finally Erin and Diane Murphy, who took over the role in 1966. Later, Erin took over the principal on-camera role due to her resemblance to Elizabeth. But if you look closely you'll see Diane in many episodes, including #178, "A Bunny for Tabatha," in which she plays Annabelle, and Episode #149, "Samantha Fights City Hall," in which she plays Tabatha. (She's on the slide in the beginning.)

What kind of tree did Darrin plant on the day Tabatha was born?

A weeping willow tree.

Who was Tabatha's baby doctor?

Dr. Koblin (Lindsay Workman) Episode #75, "Nobody's Perfect." Workman also played Darrin's doctor in the pilot.

What was the name of the doll that Santa brought Tabatha in Episode #123, "Humbug Not to be Spoken Here"?

A Suzi Bruisy doll, the only one in the world.

Adam's Oat-Currant Scones

Classic scones packed full of healthy things. Delicious with fruit jam.

½   c. Butter, chilled
2   c. Whole wheat pastry flour
1   c. Uncooked rolled oats or barley flakes
½   c. Sucanat (or ¼ c. sugar)
1   Tbs. Baking powder
½   tsp. Salt
¼   tsp. Cream of tartar
⅓   c. Soy, rice, or dairy milk
2   large Eggs
1½   tsp. Vanilla extract
½   c. Currants
½   c. Walnuts, chopped

Preheat oven to 425°F.

Cut butter into 4 pieces. Put into food processor. Add flour, oats, Sucanat, baking powder, salt, and cream of tartar. Pulse till mixture resembles coarse crumbs.

Add milk, eggs, vanilla. Pulse till combined.

Stir in currants and nuts.

Scoop out generous mounds (about ¼ cup each) onto ungreased cookie sheet.

Bake for 15 minutes. Cool 5 minutes. Serve hot or cold with jam of your choice.

YIELDS 16 TO 18.

Samantha: Actually, as long as we don't have to name the baby "Frank," there is a name I'm very fond of, "Adam."
Maurice: That was my great-grandfather's name!
Darrin: "Adam" was your great-grandfather?!!
Maurice: Not *that* "Adam"!

[Episode #176, "NAMING SAMANTHA'S NEW BABY"]

ADAM'S AFTERNOON SNACKS

Adam's Oranga-Nilla Balls

1   lb. Powdered sugar
1   stick Butter, room temperature
1   box Vanilla wafers, crushed
1   c. Walnuts, chopped
1   6-oz. can Frozen orange juice, thawed
1   tsp. Vanilla extract
1   6-oz. can Coconut, flaked (not frozen)

Cream powdered sugar and butter.
Add vanilla wafers, walnuts, orange juice, and vanilla extract.
Shape into bite-size balls and roll balls in coconut.

"The gift of beauty I give to thee,
Sweet as this flower shall you be.
Beauty is yours in mind and sight,
From baby's breath to the end of night."

Endora blesses Adam.

[Episode #176, "NAMING SAMANTHA'S NEW BABY"]

Adam's Oranga-Nilla Cooler

½   c. Vanilla yogurt
¾   c. Orange juice
2–3 drops Vanilla extract
2   Ice cubes

Blend in blender. Serving for one.

"Hear these words, oh, newborn child
On whom the universe has smiled.
With this flower, I do shed,
The gift of laughter on thy head."

Maurice showers Adam with a blessing only he can give.

[Episode #176, "NAMING SAMANTHA'S NEW BABY"]

✳ More Sugar and Spice and a Spinach Sundae ✳

Melted Witches

Endora felt these were in bad taste until she actually tasted one herself!

Pistachio ice cream
Sugar ice cream cones (the pointy ones)
Raisins
Root beer or cola

Place scoop of ice cream in each bowl. Top with sugar cone, pointy end sticking up for witch's hat. Place two raisins in ice-cream scoop for eyes.

Pour root beer or cola into bowl. Eat quickly before the witches melt away.

Endora: Most grandparents get to spend weekends with their grandchildren.
Samantha: Most grandparents don't have grandchildren who can turn them into toads!

Samantha tries explaining to Endora why she can't let Tabatha stay at Mr. and Mrs. Stephens' house for the weekend.

[Episode #163, "TABATHA'S WEEKEND"]

Tabatha's "Happy Face" Raisin Cookies

On a weekend visit at her mortal grandparents, Tabatha turned herself into a raisin cookie to avoid the bickering of Phyllis, Endora, Frank, and Samantha.

[Episode #163, "TABATHA'S WEEKEND"]

1½	c. Flour
½	tsp. Baking soda
1	tsp. Cinnamon
¼	tsp. Nutmeg
½	tsp. Salt
1	Egg, slightly beaten
1	c. Sugar
½	c. Butter, melted
1	Tbs. Molasses
¼	c. Milk
1½	c. Oatmeal, uncooked
¾	c. Raisins

Preheat oven to 350°F. Mix first four ingredients in large bowl. One by one, stir in remaining ingredients, except raisins.

Drop by large tablespoonfuls on unbuttered cookie sheets. Push raisins firmly into dough to form a smiley face with two eyes. Final cookie should be about 4 inches in diameter.

Bake until edges brown, about 10–12 minutes.

YIELD ABOUT 48 COOKIES.

Tabatha: Can grandmama have a cookie, too?
Endora: They're not by chance from an *Alice B. Toklas* recipe?
Phyllis: They're *my* recipe!
Endora: Then, I think I'll pass!

Endora "reigns" on Mrs. Stephens' parade with Tabatha.

[Episode #163, "TABATHA'S WEEKEND"]

Elspeth: Spinach! What child could abide the stuff?!
   She zaps up a sundae for Tabatha.
Darrin: Samantha!
Samantha: Oh, Darrin, it isn't really ice cream, it's Elspeth's Special Spinach Sundae! But, oh, how it fooled us little ones!

[Episode #122, "I Get Your Nanny, You Get My Goat"]

Nanny Elspeth's Special Spinach Sundae

After all those sweets it may be near to impossible to get your little Witchlets or Warlocks to eat their vegetables. But never fear, Nanny Elspeth's here!

2   pkg. Frozen spinach (Chopped is best, whole leaf O.K.)
1   pt. Sour cream
    Salt, to taste
    Garlic salt, to taste (Essential!)
    Mother's Mashed Potatoes
    Bacon bits, fried and crumbled (optional)
    Parmesan or Romano, grated

Cook spinach according to directions. Drain *very* well. Add 1 pint sour cream, salt, and garlic salt. Mix well. Place a scoop of warm "Mother's Mashed Potatoes" (from Samantha's chapter) in a glass sundae dish and spoon the creamed spinach liberally over the top! Crumble bacon over the top, sprinkle with the grated cheese, add a paper parasol and a spoon!

Darrin: Someday Tabatha is going to grow old and gray, and she just might want to tell her great-great-grandchildren about her Uncle Arthur, her Aunt Clara, Endora, Maurice. How is she ever going to get them to believe her?
Samantha: Simple. She'll just introduce them!
Darrin: I had to ask.

[Episode #80, "Endora Moves in for a Spell"]

More Kid Trivia:

What did Mrs. Stephens' mynah bird, Black Bart, prefer to be called?
"Mr. Marvelous"!

What was the name of the little boy and his mother that Mrs. Stephens took Tabatha and Samantha over to meet?
Gretchen and Michael Millhowser (Peggy Pope and Teddy Quinn) Episode #133, "Playmates."

Name the two fairy tales that Tabatha zapped herself into.
"Jack and the Beanstalk" and "Hansel and Gretel."

Actress Billie Hayes portrayed the mean old witch in Episode #238, "Hansel and Gretel in Samanthaland."

In what other TV series did Ms. Hayes become famous for playing a witch?
"H.R. Puffinstuf." She played "Witchipoo."

Dining with the Tates, Larry and Louise

Louise Tate

Louise was born Mary Louise Van Buren (no relation to the former President). Her parents were Martha and James Madison Van Buren of Van Buren Shoes, a prestigious firm that sold high quality ladies footwear in New York for over ninety years.

Louise grew up in Manhattan where she first met Larry Tate on a blind date.

She immediately disliked him!

Instead of marriage, Louise went on to become a Manhattan debutante and fashion model. In 1950 a talent scout for Paramount met her and, in the traditional Hollywood fairy tale, cast her in the lead role of his next picture. It stank.

COURTESY KASEY ROGERS PRIVATE COLLECTION

While doing a commercial for Barton Industries (a major client of McMann and Tate) Louise again ran into Larry. This time things clicked and they were married on July 29, 1954. Louise promptly gave up her impending stardom for the social life of the "1st Lady of Advertising."

Louise succeeded her late husband to become CEO of McMann and Tate.

Larry Tate

Lawrence Tate was born on April 4, 1916, in Denver, Colorado, where he grew up at 1432 Elm Drive. An avid ice hockey fan, he graduated with honors from Harvard and served in the Navy for three years. Upon his discharge he was hired as an account executive by family friend Howard McMann, of McMann Advertising. Larry was made a partner in September of '55, officially changing the company name to McMann and Tate.

While vacationing in Manhattan, some friends set Larry up on a blind date with Mary Louise Van Buren. He was instantly taken with her, and knew Louise felt the same. For some unknown reason Larry immediately lost contact with Louise until he saw her modeling book on his desk at work two years later. He called her agent and instantly hired her for a "Mother Jenny's Apple Pie" spot with Barton Industries and the rest is history.

Larry Tate passed away in November of 1990. At his eulogy, Larry's lifelong friend David White said: "Besides his apparent greed, Larry was a friend to all and that without him I would never have had as good a job."

Larry Tate is survived by his wife Louise and their son Jonathan.

✳ Larry and Louise's New Year's Eve Party ✳

NEW YEAR'S EVE PARTY MENU

5th Avenue BourBon Balls

Easy Street Bonbons

Tate's Date Sticks

Madison Avenue Champagne Punch for Memorable Occasions

Betty's Hors d'oeuvres

Hot Sour Cream Mushrooms

Pork on Bamboo Skewers

Clients in a Blanket

Angelic Vacation Ambrosia

Pumpkin Cheese Cake

Brandy Crêpes Suzette

5th Avenue Bourbon Balls

1¾ c. Chocolate wafers, ground
1 c. Confectioner's sugar, sifted
1¾ c. Pecans, chopped
6 Tbs. Bourbon
2 Tbs. White corn syrup
1 tsp. Cinnamon
½ tsp. Nutmeg, freshly grated
More Confectioner's sugar, sifted, for dredging candy balls

Thoroughly mix all the above ingredients, except the last. Form into 1-inch balls. Dredge (roll) them in the additional sifted confectioner's sugar.

Make up to six weeks ahead. Store in airtight containers in a cool, dry place.

YIELDS ABOUT 30 BALLS.

Easy Street Bonbons (So-o-o rich!)

1 14-oz. can Sweetened, condensed milk
1 12-oz. pkg. Semi-sweet chocolate pieces
6 Tbs. Cocoa
4 Tbs. Butter
6 Tbs. Brandy
Additional cocoa for coating

Pour the condensed milk into a saucepan, heat to boiling, lower the heat and cook for 7 minutes, stirring frequently.

Add the chocolate, cocoa, butter, and brandy. Cook for 5 additional minutes, stirring occasionally.

Allow to cool to room temperature. Form small balls with moist hands. Roll in cocoa powder and place in individual frilly paper cups (like petit fours).

Chill for at least two hours before serving.
YIELD 1 POUND.

Tate's Date Sticks

This recipe is over 60 years old. It comes from Mark's grandmother, Janet Keagle.

> 3   **Eggs, well beaten**
> 1   **c. Sugar**
> 1   **c. Flour**
> 1   **c. Dates**
> 1   **c. Nuts (pecans, walnuts, whatever)**
> ½   **tsp. Baking powder**

Beat eggs in a bowl. Add all other ingredients. Mix well.

Preheat oven to 350°F. Grease and flour square pan. Bake ingredients in pan until they are light brown and spring back at the touch. Cool.

Cut into strips and roll in XXXX sugar.

Madison Avenue Champagne Punch for Memorable Occasions

(Serves 50, if you use champagne glasses.)
In your prettiest large punch bowl, pour:

> 2   bottles Dom Perignon Champagne*
> 1   large bottle Sauterne

Mix:

> 1   c. Sugar
> 2   c. Lemon juice (in bottle)
> 1   12-oz. can Pineapple chunks, drained
> 1   large pkg. Frozen strawberries

Add sugar, lemon juice, pineapple chunks, and frozen strawberries to wine in punch bowl and blend.

Add Gigantic Ice Cube. (Instructions follow.) Chill and serve.

Suggest you have plenty of refill ingredients on hand. This goes fast!

Gigantic Ice Cube

Prepare ahead. I use this in all punch bowls and always make two or three.

> **Water**
> **Fresh strawberries**
> **Pineapple chunks (if desired)**

*Between you and me, leave one bottle of Dom Perignon standing in full view of your guests, but *don't* waste it in punch. Use less expensive champagne. A *lot* less expensive. They'll never know.

Pour water into very large bowl or square container. Add fresh strawberries and pineapple. Freeze in advance.
Note:
For Halloween, instead of fresh fruit, I freeze black plastic spiders and flies, strips of red bell pepper for coagulated blood, and chunks of papaya or yellow melon for . . . never mind. Use your imagination.

"Today the Nation . . . tomorrow, the world! I've wanted to rule the world ever since I was a little kid!"

During a spell-induced dream, Darrin sees what it would be like to tell Larry that Samantha's a witch.

[Episode #135, "I CONFESS"]

BETTY'S HORS D' OEUVRES

Betty could do a good deal more than just type and take dictation! She knew how to "burn"! Er . . . "cook," that is. Her hors d' oeurves were the hit of every occasion whether it was New Year's Eve or an important client dinner. Thanks, Betty.

—Louise

Hot Sour Cream Mushrooms

1   lb. Mushrooms
1   Tbs. Butter
1   clove Garlic
½   tsp. Salt
1   Tbs. Lemon juice
1   Tbs. Dill weed (or, to taste)
¼   tsp. Pepper
    Sherry. Start with 1 Tbs. and keep going till it suits your taste.
1   c. Sour cream

Wash and dry mushrooms. Melt butter and add crushed garlic. To mushrooms, add all ingredients except sour cream. Cook approximately 20 minutes.

Pour small amount of liquid in sour cream and blend. Pour sour cream over mushrooms and blend. Refrigerate overnight.

Serve hot with fancy crackers.

Pork on Bamboo Skewers

2	lbs. Pork loin, cut into thin strips about 1 inch wide.
4	cloves Garlic, minced
¾	c. Soy sauce
10	oz. Dijon mustard
½	c. Honey

Mix together all except pork. Taste. Adjust mixture to your taste. Set aside ½ for dipping later.

Pour the other half over the pork strips and marinate for at least 30 minutes in refrigerator.

Weave pork strips onto bamboo skewers and discard marinade.

Broil 3–4 minutes. Serve hot with reserved sauce.
SERVES 4.

Clients in a Blanket

Easy.

1	pkg. Croissant dough, defrosted (available frozen in supermarket)
1	pkg. Precooked frozen sausage links

Cut dough into triangles and place a whole or half sausage link in wide end of triangle and roll tightly, sealing the ends.

Bake in preheated oven according to directions on package of dough.

Serve piping hot with a little mustard for dipping.

"Darrin, if I've told you once, I've told you a thousand times, integrity doesn't feed the bulldog!"

[Another Larry-ism. Episode #181, "DARRIN THE WARLOCK"]

"I didn't become the president of McMann and Tate without bending my integrity occasionally, and this is one of those occasionallys!"

[A Larry-ism. Episode #224, "OUT OF THE MOUTHS OF BABES"]

"I didn't get to be the head of an advertising agency without stretching the truth now and then. I might honestly say, I'm one of the best truth stretchers in the business!"

[Yet another Larry-ism, this one from Episode #128, "HIPPIE, HIPPIE HOORAY"]

Samantha: Larry, you need a rest. You and Louise should take a little vacation.
Larry: You mean from each other?

[Episode #226, "SAMANTHA'S MAGIC MIRROR"]

Angelic Vacation Ambrosia

Ambrosia started out as sliced orange sections sprinkled with coconut and chilled.

Then someone added sliced bananas.

My favorite melt-in-your-mouth concoction is equal parts of:

Orange sections (fresh or canned mandarin)
Pineapple tidbits (fresh or canned, drained)
Sliced bananas
Tiny marshmallows

Mix thoroughly. (May add the smallest amount of pineapple juice, but not really necessary. The marshmallows dissolve slightly giving a nice consistency.)

Sprinkle with shredded coconut, and chill well before serving.

DESSERTS

Pumpkin Cheese Cake

Crust

1⅓   c. Gingersnap crumbs
½   stick Melted butter

Mix gingersnap crumbs and butter well and then press into 8-inch spring form.

Bake at 350°F. for 10 minutes.

Cool completely before filling.

Filling

2   8-oz. pkgs. Cream cheese
2   c. Pumpkin (canned or fresh)
¾   c. Brown sugar, firmly packed
2   tsp. Cornstarch
1   tsp. Cinnamon
½   tsp. Ground nutmeg
½   tsp. Ground ginger

Blend all ingredients thoroughly. Pour into crust and bake at 350°F. until inserted toothpick comes out clean. Remove from oven and cool completely (4 hours). Refrigerate until ready to serve.

Brandy Crêpes Suzette

Famous French dessert.

½ c. Enriched flour
½ tsp. Baking powder, double-acting
½ tsp. Salt
1 c. Milk
2 Eggs, slightly beaten
½ tsp. Lemon zest (grated rind)

Sift dry ingredients.

Add milk and slightly beaten eggs. Stir until just mixed. Do not over mix. Batter must be *very* thin.

Melt a dab of butter in small nonstick skillet over direct heat. Pour in small amount of batter and twirl around pan so the batter covers the entire surface. Turn, but only once.

When brown, roll, place in chafing dish and cover with Crêpes Suzette Brandy Sauce (follows).

YIELDS 10 TO 11.

Crêpes Suzette Brandy Sauce

½ c. Butter
½ c. Confectioner's sugar, sifted
¼ c. Brandy
1 Orange, juice and grated rind

Mix and then heat all ingredients. Pour over rolled pancakes.

✳ New Year's Day Brunch Tradition ✳

MENU
Aunt Harriet's Hoppin' John
Aunt Millicent's Captivating Collard Greens
Hot Southern Corn Bread
Specter Apple Crisp

✳

New Year's Day

Start the New Year right!

Aunt Harriet's Hoppin' John

Aunt Harriet (Nellie Burt), poor dear, still thinks she can conjure up the afterlife and spirit world, but has finally given up her crystal ball in favor of the Ouija board. Personally I don't believe it, but Aunt Harriet keeps telling me she's talking to someone named Uncle Willie (Harry Harvey, #134)!

1	c. Black-eyed peas
	Water to cover, plus 6 cups
6–8	slices Bacon
1	large Onion, chopped
2	cloves Garlic, minced
	Butter

Barely cover black-eyed peas with cold water and boil for 2 or 3 minutes.

Cover with lid and let stand 1 to 4 hours to shorten cooking time.

Now add 6 cups of water and cook at a simmer for an hour or until done. (Check package for any specific directions.)

Sauté bacon, onions, and garlic in butter. When golden, stir in cooked black-eyed peas.

Serve with Collard Greens, hot Southern Corn Bread, and butter.

YIELDS 4 CUPS.

Aunt Millicent's Captivating Collard Greens

Just thought I'd let y'all know, Aunt Millicent (Ruth McDevitt) finally got over Grover Stephens . . . You remember him? Darrin's grandfather (#210). She started dating one of Larry's clients soon after.

1	Ham bone with some meat attached
¼–½	lb. Salt pork, cubed
6	c. Water
3	lbs. Collard greens
	Salt, to taste
	Pepper, to taste
	Dash Cayenne (optional)

Boil the ham bone and salt pork for 45 minutes.

Carefully wash the collard greens. Remove tough ends and chop the rest.

Add greens to the pot with the ham bone, and continue cooking until tender (about another 45 minutes.) Both water and salt pork will almost have disappeared.

Add any meat from the bone to the greens and discard bone. Salt and pepper to taste. A dash or two of cayenne will add spark.

SERVES 6.

Louise: What did that hound's-tooth sports jacket represent to Darrin?

Samantha: Bad taste?

Louise: Too simple! According to Dr. Kramer, the way a husband or wife feels about how a spouse dresses shows the condition of the entire relationship!

Louise plays psychiatrist to Samantha. Good thing Endora decided to bring in an expert and conjured up Sigmund Freud (Norman Fell).

[Episode #84, "I'D RATHER TWITCH THAN FIGHT"]

Hot Southern Corn Bread

2½	c. Yellow corn meal
1½	c. Flour
1½	tsp. Baking powder
½	tsp. Salt
¼	c. Sugar
4	oz. Plain sour cream
1	Egg
½	c. Milk
4	Tbs. Butter or bacon fat
½	c. Broccoli, chopped
½	c. Cheddar cheese, shredded
½	medium Onion, diced
4	Tbs. Green chilis, canned and chopped (optional)

Preheat oven to 350°F.

Mix all the dry ingredients. In separate bowl, beat the egg, and add milk and bacon fat. Pour liquids into dry ingredients, and mix gently *only* until smooth. (Do not overbeat.) Gently fold in the rest of the ingredients.

Grease 9-inch square pan or big old iron skillet. Bake 30 to 40 minutes or until golden brown.

YIELDS 22–23 2-INCH SQUARES.

✳   ✳   ✳

The Knees Have It: In 1966, when I joined *Bewitched,* Elizabeth wore her skirts at knee length. Miniskirts were beginning to be fashionable, but Liz vowed she would never shorten her skirts. Check out subsequent episodes. They got shorter and shorter showing off her fabulous legs.

✳   ✳   ✳

Specter Apple Crisp

1   c. Orange juice
4   c. Granny Smith apples, peeled and sliced
1   c. Sugar
¾   c. All-purpose flour, sifted
1   tsp. Cinnamon
½   tsp. Nutmeg
   Salt, to taste
⅓   c. Butter
   Whipping cream (optional)

Put the orange juice in a large bowl and slice apples into the juice to keep them from turning brown and to keep moist. Set aside.

In another bowl combine sugar, flour, cinnamon, nutmeg, and salt. Cut butter into small pieces and add to mixture. With pastry blender continue to cut butter into mixture until a uniformly coarse texture.

Remove sliced apples from orange juice and place on buttered pie plate, building a mound in the center. Remeasure orange juice. If more than ¾ cup remains, spoon orange juice over apples until only ¾ cup juice is left. Sprinkle coarse crumb mixture evenly over apples.

In preheated 375°F. oven, bake 45 to 50 minutes. Topping should be browned and apples tender.

Best when served warm with whipped cream.
SERVES 4 TO 5.

Larry: Louise, you had better tell us, because if you don't we'll start imagining something ridiculous, like he was making a pass at you!

Louise: And why is that so ridiculous?

Larry: (Laughing) Well, because you're old enough to be Darrin's—

Louise: Don't say it!

Larry: Why not . . . ? Sister!

Darrin, possessed by a woman-hungry spook, makes a pass at Louise. The perplexed Louise tries to talk some sense into him, to no avail. The blushing Louise comes back inside the castle, not knowing what to say. As usual, Larry doesn't help.

[Episode #235, "THE GHOST WHO MADE A SPECTER OF HIMSELF"]

✳ Luncheon with Louise ✳

"The wife of an advertising czar like Larry has to do more than just look good, let me tell you! She has to run the household, take care of the children, entertain the clients. In fact, if it weren't for Samantha and me, some clients would've slipped right through McMann *and* Tate's fingers. So, while Larry and Darrin handle the men, I'll show you what it takes to win the ladies over and *cinch* their accounts."

[—Louise]

LADIES' LUNCHEON MENU

Evelyn Tucker's Nutty Apricot Bread

with

Slivers of Ham

Cora May's Tossed Spinach and Chicken Salad

Adrienne Sebastian's Garlic Bread

Madame Maruska's Fat Man's Pie

Endora: Do you think boots will be popular next season?
Terry: I guess that depends on how well "Boots" behaves herself this season!

Fashion designer Terry Warbell (Julie Gregg) doesn't seem to know what Endora's talking about. Could it be she's actually the 500-year-old "Crone of Cawdor"?

[EPISODE #101]

"When Your Man Uses Brawn Cologne, There's No Telling How Wild He Might get!"

Samantha's slogan for Brawn Cologne.

[Episode #162, "GOING APE"]

Evelyn Tucker's Nutty Apricot Bread with Slivers of Ham

"When Evelyn Tucker (Gail Kobe) hired Harry Simian (Lou Antonio) for a commercial spot, she didn't know he would make a monkey out of her and wreck the entire shoot! Luckily Samantha saved the day for Larry and Darrin when she came up with the award-winning slogan for Brawn Cologne."

¾	c. Apricots, dried, chopped
¼	c. Currants, dried (or more, if desired)
2	Tbs. Butter, unsalted, softened
1	c. Light brown sugar, firmly packed
1	large Egg
¾	c. Milk
¾	c. Fresh orange juice
1	Tbs. Orange zest (grated orange rind)
3	c. All-purpose flour
3½	tsp. Baking powder, double-acting
¼	tsp. Baking soda

Few dashes Salt
¾ **c. Pecans, chopped**
1 **c. Boiling water**

Combine apricots and currants with 1 cup of boiling water. Let stand for 20 minutes and drain.

In separate bowl, cream together butter and brown sugar until light and fluffy. Beat in egg, milk, orange juice, and rind. Beat until smooth.

In another small bowl, sift together the flour, baking powder, baking soda, and salt. Beat this into the brown sugar mixture. Stir in pecans, apricots, and currants.

Divide into two well-buttered loaf pans. Bake in a preheated 350°F. oven.

Cool 10 minutes. Loosen edges and remove to rack to cool completely.

Serve with softened butter and thin slices of smoked ham or turkey.

"Don't Be Messy, Messy, Buy a Cora May Dressy-Wessy!"

Cora May Franklin (Sara Seegar)

[Episode #254, "THE TRUTH, NOTHING BUT THE TRUTH, SO HELP ME, SAM"]

Cora May's Tossed Spinach and Chicken Salad

After Larry and Darrin insulted Cora May at Samantha's house (Episode #254), it took me two luncheons of her favorite Spinach and Chicken Salad, plus a lot of the old "McMann and Tact" to convince her that her own slogan really did stink!

1	lb. Spinach
3	Tbs. Lemon juice (Fresh is best.)
5	Tbs. Olive oil
1–2	cloves Garlic, minced
2	tsp. Dijon mustard
½	lb. Mushrooms, sliced thinly
	Salt, to taste
	Pepper, to taste
2 or 3	Chicken breasts, cut into chunks

Soak the spinach in cold water. Rinse each leaf well under cold running water. Discard any thick stems. Pat dry.

In large salad bowl, combine the lemon juice, oil, garlic, and mustard. Add sliced mushrooms and toss, coating with dressing.

Add spinach and toss well. Season to taste with salt and pepper.

Add chicken chunks and serve.

Variation: May substitute crumbled bacon and hard-boiled eggs, quartered, for chicken.

SERVES 2 TO 3.

"I want a campaign that says: You've got two choices. Use Adrienne Sebastian Products . . . or be ugly!"

Adrienne Sebastian's (Mala Powers) right-hand man, Mr. Traynor (Herbert Voland), cuts to the chase.

[Episode #153, "INSTANT COURTESY"]

Adrienne Sebastian's Garlic Bread

Cosmetic companies always need a woman's touch, and Mr. Traynor certainly could have used it too! It's a good thing that Mrs. Sebastian went with Darrin's idea of using a more feminine campaign than the old "hard sell" approach. Men!

Long loaf of French bread cut lengthwise.

Mix:

> 1   **stick Butter, melted**
> 2   **large cloves Garlic, minced**
>   **Parmesan cheese, grated**
>   **Paprika**

Spread cut sides of bread with butter and garlic. Sprinkle with Parmesan cheese; dust lightly with paprika for color. Broil until toasted.

"Don't Play Fair, Use Madame Maruska's Lipstick!"
After wrongly accusing Madame Maruska (Lisa Kirk) of being an impostor, Samantha saved the day by authorizing McMann and Tate to print this slogan in all the newspapers.

> [Episode #104, "How To Fail in Business with all Kinds of Help"]

Madame Maruska's Fat Man's Pie

To be perfectly honest, Madame Maruska or rather, "That's Ma-ROOSH-KA!" as she would shout, loves to fatten up her clients right before she gives them the ax! Obviously Maruska doesn't cook, but I thought this recipe suited her just fine.

First Layer:

> 1   **stick Butter**
> 1   **c. Flour, plain**
> ½   **c. Pecans, chopped**

Melt butter. Blend with flour and nuts. Press mixture into bottom of glass baking dish. Bake at 350°F. for 20 minutes. Cool.

Second Layer:

> 8 oz. Cream cheese
> 1 c. Cool Whip
> 1 c. Powdered sugar

Blend and spread over first layer.

Third Layer:

> 1 small pkg. Instant chocolate pudding
> 1 small pkg. Instant vanilla pudding
> 3⅓ c. Cold milk

Using ½ the milk for each pudding, mix the puddings in separate bowls. Spread the vanilla. Then spread the chocolate.

Fourth Layer:

Top with Cool Whip. Garnish with nuts or chocolate chips, or both, if desired.

Calories don't count if no one's looking.

✳ Tête à Tate Candlelight Dinner ✳

MENU

Champagne

Mimosa Cocktails and Variations

Raven Cordon Bleu

Give In to Green Beans

McMann and Torch

Champagne Cocktail

1	oz. Cognac
½	oz. Grand Marnier
6	oz. Champagne, chilled
3	Raspberries per drink, garnish

In crystal tulip or champagne flute pour cognac, followed by Grand Marnier, followed by chilled champagne. Garnish with raspberries.

Champagne Variations

To champagne, add one perfect strawberry with stem.
Or, add a dash of raspberry syrup and a spoonful of raspberries.
Float blueberries or blackberries.

Mimosas

Champagne
Orange juice
Fresh mint

Fill crystal tulip or champagne flute ⅔ full with champagne. Top off with ⅓ orange juice. Garnish with sprig of fresh mint.

Rogers and Hammer-Sling: We were shooting on a "swing-set," our regular dressing rooms on another stage. The crew had put up shaky old canvas siding, creating makeshift rooms. No closets, no tables. Not even a cot or chair. I happened to be wearing my new (and first) mink coat in the scene, and I remarked to Elizabeth that I had no place to hang the coat. Five minutes later a crew member walked in and hammered a huge 6-penny nail in a support post. He said, "There ya go. Sling it on that!"

* * *

Raven Cordon Bleu

Ravens' breasts are a bit tough and hard to come by, so I substitute chicken breasts.

    Chicken breasts, one or more per person
    Cheese—Gruyère, Provolone, or mozzarella
4   **thin slices Ham, per chicken breast**
4   **Tbs. Butter, melted, or more**
½   **c. Bread crumbs, or more**
1   **pinch Paprika**
    Salt

Flatten chicken breast. Place slices of cheese and ham on top of chicken.

Roll up chicken with cheese and ham inside.

Roll stuffed chicken in butter, then crumbs. Place on buttered baking dish.

Season with paprika and salt.

Bake at 400°F. for 40 minutes.

"The hardest thing for him to give is in!"

> Samantha tells it like it is about Larry in
> Episode #138, "THE NO-HARM CHARM."

Give In to Green Beans

2   **lbs. Green beans, trimmed and cut into 1-inch pieces**
3   **Tbs. Butter, unsalted**
1   **tsp. Lemon zest (grated rind)**
1   **Tbs. Fresh rosemary leaves, minced**
    Salt, to taste
    Pepper, to taste

Cover beans with boiling water and cook for 5 minutes. Remove from heat. Drain and rinse immediately. Beans should be green and crisp. (This can be done ahead, if desired.)

At serving time:

In a small saucepan, melt butter over low heat with the lemon zest, rosemary, salt, and pepper.

Reheat beans. Transfer to serving dish and add the butter mixture.

SERVES 7.

McMann and Torch

Simple, spectacular, but handle with care.

For a simple, but dramatic dessert, place a single scoop of vanilla ice cream in a stemmed, crystal, wide champagne glass.

✳ Will the real Louise Tate please stand up?

More McMann and Trivia

He only appeared in two episodes and was played by someone different each time, but what was McMann's first name?
Howard. Once played by great character actor Leon Ames, better known as Judy Garland's father in *Meet Me in St. Louis.*

What regular Bewitched client wrote an episode?
Arthur Julian wrote Episode #148, "Is It Magic or Imagination?"

What was the ultimate name of the perfume that client Mr. Cunningham (Arthur Julian) decided on?
"I Know You." It was his favorite phrase.

What Bewitched regular directed an episode?
David (Larry Tate) White, himself. Episode #182, "Samantha's Double Mother Trouble"

Pour crème de menthe over ice cream. (Or Frangelico or brandy or your favorite liqueur.) Top each scoop with a sugar cube soaked in alcohol (rum, brandy, liqueur, etc.).

At serving time, dim all the lights and light all of the sugar cubes. They will burn festively and die out just in time to enjoy.

Louise: Larry! You're in Chicago!
Larry: No I'm not, the flight was delayed.
Louise: How'd you get Jonathan?
Larry: The stork brought him!

After seeing Sam take Jonathan upstairs for his sweater, Louise runs into Larry carrying Jonathan out of the kitchen! It's another one of Aunt Clara's magic mess-ups when she splits Jonathan into two children in

Episode #78, "Accidental Twins."

The Kravitz Kitchen
Gladys and Abner

Gladys and Abner Kravitz

Gladys Gruber was born in Poughkeepsie, New York, which she constantly mispronounced "Kapoopsie." Her family founded Poughkeepsie Woolens in which she is the major stock holder. Gladys has one brother, Louis, whom she adores. Louis was a prodigy on the violin until he lost his knickers on stage at the tender age of nine.

Abner Kravitz hailed from New York's Lower East Side. He met Gladys in college, where he proposed to her over an ice cream soda. They spent their honeymoon on the SS *Sorrento.*

It sank!

Abner once remarked that, "All the time we were floating in the ocean, I felt someone was trying to tell me something!" Today, Abner Kravitz resides on the family mantel in an ornate urn.

Since Abner's death in February of 1980, Gladys has become a published author. Her first book, "The Samantha Stephens I Have Known and Feared" came to her in a dream and was on the New York Times bestseller list for 8 years. Her next two books, "Sex, Pots and Pans" and "Always Say Maybe" (a girl's guide to dating) followed soon after. Both books were published under the nom de plume of Sandra Gould.

Mrs. Kravitz would like everyone to know that her recipe for chicken soup has cured over four hundred and sixty-eight sick friends and relatives in the last forty years.

Mr. and the two Mrs. Kravitzes.
(George Tobias, Sandra Gould,
and Alice Pearce)

COURTESY STEVE COX COLLECTION

COURTESY STEVE COX COLLECTION

✳ Abner's Favorite Dinner ✳

Abner: I never thought I'd beg to eat her cooking!

[Episode #29, "ABNER KADABRA"]

MENU

Gladys' Ten-Pound Meat Loaf

Westport Green Beans

Diced Carrots and Turnips

Ed Wright's Campaign Cobbler

or

Pleasure's Peachy-Keen Neighborly Yogurt

Gladys' Ten-Pound Meat Loaf

"I always say, the way to a man's heart, without driving a "steak" into it, is always meat loaf. Here is my version of a ten-pound meat loaf."

[—Sandra Gould]

5	lbs. Ground chuck
5	lbs. Ground turkey
2	medium Onions, chopped
2	large Eggs
1	tsp. Salt (Optional, but I never season with salt.)
2	Tbs. Garlic salt
½	c. Milk
1	c. Water
1	tsp. Pepper
1	c. Catsup (or spaghetti sauce)
1	box Mushrooms, sliced and fresh
	Butter

In a wooden bowl, combine meat, onions, eggs, salt, garlic salt, milk, water, pepper, and catsup. Mix very well, then shape into long mound on a large flat Pyrex dish or casserole.

Bake in preheated oven at 300°F. for an hour.

Put fork through to see if it's finished.

Slice mushrooms and sauté in butter until almost transparent.

Ten minutes before serving, pour mushrooms on top of meat loaf and cook another fifteen minutes.

The oohs and ahhs will make him forget the diamond bracelet he's about to spend thousands for.*

SERVES 20.

*Exact recipe as contributed by "Gladys Kravitz" herself.

Maurice Who? When I was a young girl, going to Dramatic School, I saw Maurice Evans perform. I sat in the front row at all these Shakespearean things. Then, when he did *Bewitched* and I had a big scene with him, I suddenly realized that I was working with the great Maurice Evans I had seen when I was a child. I forgot all of my lines! I forgot everything! I just stood there and looked at him, then said "I'm working with you, I can't believe it!" And he said, "Child, I'm not that important. You're just as important." Which, I thought, was nice.

[—S.G.]

Kravitz Trivia

George Tobias once starred opposite James Cagney, Rita Hayworth, Olivia De Havilland and TV's Superman, George Reeves in what black-and-white classic?
  The Strawberry Blonde (available at fine video stores near you!)

Sandra Gould made what radio role famous?
  Miss Duffy in "Duffy's Tavern"

What Doris Day movie gave the producers of Bewitched *the idea of neighbors Gladys and Abner Kravitz?*
  The Glass Bottom Boat in which Alice Pearce and George Tobias co-starred

How long has Abner loved Gladys?
  "Since she fell off the truck on my fraternity hayride!"

    [—Abner Kravitz, Episode #32, "Illegal Separation"]

Westport Green Beans

2 pkgs. Green beans (Julienne is nice.)
1 can Cream of mushroom soup
½ c. Milk
½ pkg. Almonds, sliced

Cook green beans according to directions on box. Servings are specified.

Drain. Mix mushroom soup and milk. Pour over green beans. Sprinkle with sliced almonds.

Bake at 350°F. for 15 minutes or warm on stove top in large skillet.

Diced Carrots and Turnips

2 lbs. Carrots, diced (½-inch cubes)
1½ lb. Turnips, peeled and diced (½-inch cubes)
3 Tbs. Butter, unsalted
   Nutmeg, to taste, fresh grated
   Salt, to taste
   Pepper, to taste

In kettle of boiling salted water, cook carrots 3 minutes.
Add turnips and boil another 3 to 5 minutes or until tender.
Drain veggies and transfer to serving dish.
Add butter cut into bits, nutmeg, salt, and pepper.
Toss to melt butter and serve.
SERVES 11 TO 12.

Abner and Gladys
"Rally for Wright"
in Episode #34,
"Remember the Main"

Ed Wright's Campaign Cobbler

2½	lb. Peaches, peeled, cored, and sliced
2	tsp. Orange peel, grated
1	Navel orange, peeled and sectioned
¼	c. Orange juice
2	Tbs. Lemon juice
¼	c. Honey
¼	c. Brown sugar, firmly packed
1½	Tbs. Flour
½	tsp. Cinnamon
2	Tbs. Butter, diced
	Melted butter for brushing biscuits

First, go next door and borrow a cup of sugar so you can snoop on what's happening at the neighbors! Next, divide it into fourths and put ¾ of it aside!

Combine the peaches and remaining ingredients, except for the melted butter, in a large bowl. Cover and let stand while you prepare the biscuit dough.

Biscuit dough

1½	c. All-purpose flour
1	Tbs. Sugar
2	tsp. Baking powder
½	tsp. Salt
6	Tbs. Butter, diced
3–4	Tbs. Milk

Sift together all dry ingredients. Cut in the butter until the mixture looks like coarse meal. Toss with the milk and form into a ball. Pat the dough on a floured board until it is round and about ¼ inch thick.

With 2-inch biscuit cutter dipped in flour, cut biscuits.

Now pour or spoon the peach mixture into a deep 9-inch baking pan. Arrange the biscuits over the peaches, overlapping slightly.

Brush the biscuits with melted butter and bake in preheated 375°F. oven until golden and bubbling, about 50 or 60 minutes.

YIELDS 10 TO 12.

Dish up with lightly whipped cream if desired. Take back next door and share with the neighbors! Save rest of sugar for another recipe.

Thor "Thunderbolt" Swenson: Do you have "Pleasure" in this house?
Abner: Not too often, but occasionally.

[Episode #25, "Pleasure O'Reilly"]

Pleasure's Peachy-Keen Neighborly Yogurt

Darrin found this recipe floating around "Pleasure" O'Reilly's (Kipp Hamilton) kitchen while trying to fix her dishwasher. Since she had just moved in and swore she didn't know how to cook, he figured it must have been left by the previous family that had lived in the house. A family named Baxter who had a maid named Hazel! (See Trivia on page 111)

1	env. Unflavored gelatin
1	c. Skim milk
½	c. Sugar
	Dash Salt
2½	c. Vanilla low-fat yogurt
2	tsp. Vanilla extract
3	c. Frozen peaches, pureed

Sprinkle gelatin over milk in saucepan. Let stand one minute. Cook over low heat stirring constantly until gelatin dissolves.

Remove from heat and add half a cup of sugar and the salt, stirring until sugar dissolves.

Stir in yogurt, vanilla, and pureed peaches. Cover and chill.

After a while, put in individual dishes, and put in freezer for 2½ hours. Ready to serve. Yields about 7½ cups at 82 calories a serving.

This will make the angels sing and Kitchen Witches arrive on their broomsticks to invade your kitchen!

[—Gladys]

Abner: Gladys, let's play house. You be the door and I'll shut you!

[Episode #184, "SANTA COMES TO VISIT
AND STAYS AND STAYS"]

✳ **4th of July Bar B Que** ✳

MENU

Gladys' Civil War Fruit Punch

*S.S. **Sorrento** Pastrami Dip*

Hogersdorf's Hot Dogs

Connecticut Corn on the Cob

Gruber's Unbelievable Strawberry Short Cake

Abner's Proposal Banana Split

Gladys: Why can't you get your nose out of that dumb book?
Abner: I want to see how it ends.
Gladys: It's about the Civil War, the North won!
Abner: Thank you, Gladys.

[Episode #152, "Weep No More, My Willow"]

Gladys' Civil War Fruit Punch

(Nonalcoholic.)

1   c. Water
2   c. Sugar

Boil 5 minutes. Add:

1   c. Strong tea
2   c. Fruit syrup (Strawberry or loganberry from market.)
1   c. Lemon juice (in bottle)
2   c. Orange juice
2   c. Pineapple juice

Let stand 30 minutes. Then, add:

4   qts. Ice water
1   c. Maraschino cherries
1   qt. Soda water

Pour over Gigantic Ice Cube in punch bowl and serve.
SERVES 50.

You Get My Goat! In one particular episode (#115, "The Safe and Sane Halloween") a goat fell in love with me! "Louise, the goat." It was a *he,* though. During a break in shooting, I had to go to the ladies room, and all of a sudden I looked down and there was Louise (the goat, *not* Tate!) in the cubicle with me! He had followed me all the way to the ladies room!

[—S.G.]

S.S. Sorrento Pastrami Dip

Abner and Gladys never forgot the *sinking* feeling they had on their honeymoon, when their ship didn't come in! So, in honor of the less than happy event, the Kravitzes invite you to *sink* your teeth into this delectable morsel. Nibble it along with the punch.

Buy large round loaf of French bread. Cut off top ⅓ of loaf. Scoop out the soft white center leaving ½-inch shell and top.

Tear soft bread into bite-size pieces and store in airtight, plastic bag until serving time.

    4   c. Sour cream
   24   oz. Cream cheese
   10   oz. Pastrami (Turkey pastrami works well, too.)
    8   dashes Worcestershire sauce
    2   Tbs. Green onions, chopped
    ½   c. Green peppers, chopped finely
    ¼   tsp. Garlic

Mix all above ingredients well, and fill bottom of French bread loaf to the brim. Place top of bread on. Wrap entire loaf in foil.
Bake at 250°F. for 2 hours.

At serving time, place loaf in center of tray. Surround with the chunks of bread for dipping. When out of white bread, tear lid and continue "Sinking into the Sorrento"!

Gladys: My butcher who looks like Henry Fonda wants to date me!

Hogersdorf's Hot Dogs

May be chicken, turkey, or regular hot dogs.
Place on grill. Turn often until browned or skin splits.
Serve in warmed hot dog buns with choice of condiments—mustard, mayo, catsup, relish, etc.

Hogersdorf's Buns

Wrap all in aluminum foil and warm at edge of grill.
"Kravitz, you might as well know now, I'm madly in love with your wife! I've been in love with her since the first day she walked into my shop and asked if my chickens were healthy!"

[—Mr. Leon Hogersdorf (Arthur Julian), the Butcher.
Previous from Episode #140, "SPLITSVILLE"]

Abner: You've called the police department, the fire department, and the SPCA! Who are you calling now? How many people have to tell you you're crazy?
Gladys: Councilman Green? This is Gladys Kravitz, the chairwoman of the neighborhood committee for your reelection!
Abner: Crazy, but shrewd!

[Episode #81, "TWITCH OR TREAT"]

Connecticut Corn on the Cob

Gladys' only memory of her brief sojourn to seventeenth-century Plymouth was of how to fix corn on the cob on an open grill. Still rattled by that fateful trip, though, she refuses to celebrate Thanksgiving anymore!

Select corn with full husks.
Pull husks apart slightly at top and drop a spoonful of water on corn. Close tops tightly.
Roast on grill 20 minutes or more, turning occasionally.
Corn will be exceptionally sweet.
Have plenty of butter and napkins on hand.

Gruber's Unbelievable Old-Fashioned Strawberry Shortcake

Back when Gladys was a little girl, shortcake was made with biscuit dough and served with unsweetened heavy cream, unwhipped.

Heat oven to 425°F. Butter a 9-inch, round cake pan. Sift together:

2	c. Flour
1	tsp. Baking powder
½	tsp. Salt
⅓	c. Sugar
	Dash Nutmeg

Blend ingredients with fork. Then add:

⅓ **c. Butter**
1 **Egg, beaten**
⅓ **c. Milk (or a tad more)**

Add butter and blend. Add egg and blend. Add milk and blend slowly until the dough holds together but is still soft.

Flour board and divide dough into 2 parts. Roll out into 9-inch rounds. Put one round in the pan. Spread lightly with:

2 **Tbs. Butter, melted**

Place the second half on top. Bake 12 minutes. Split carefully with a fork and brush lightly with more butter.

1 **qt. Strawberries**
Sugar

"I believed she was a Witch from the second I met her! The problem is, you didn't believe me!"

—So says Gladys to Abner in a dream sequence where Darrin has decided to tell the world about Samantha's "Witchly Wife-Craft"!

[Episode #135, "I CONFESS"]

COURTESY SANDRA GOULD PRIVATE COLLECTION

Set aside a few whole berries for garnish.

In a glass or Pyroceram pot, lightly crush all the rest. Add sugar to taste and warm slightly.

Spread between layers and on top of the shortcake. Add whole berries.

Serve with heavy cream (whipped or not). Whipped cream instruction follows.

Whipped Cream

½ **pt. Heavy cream**
4 **Tbs. Sugar**

Begin whipping with electric beater on high. As cream thickens, sprinkle in sugar and whip more slowly. Stop before it turns to butter. Ladle on shortcake and berries. Top with whole berries and go for it. To die for.

Shortcake Shortcut

Witchcraft may be a fascinating way to take a shortcut, but it isn't the only way! Here's how the mortals do it!

Buy one of those packages of four ready-made shortcakes (usually in the produce department by the strawberries).

Prepare strawberries as above. Spoon liberally over individual shortcakes, and top with Whipped Cream. (Freshly made is better, but you can use the whipped cream you buy in the spray containers in the dairy department of your market.)

Gladys: I want him to want to come home! I want him to get on his hands and knees and say that he can't live without me!
Samantha: What if he's too stubborn to admit it?
Gladys: I'll kill him!

[Episode #32, "ILLEGAL SEPARATION"]

Abner's Proposal Banana Split

Few people realized that Abner was a true romantic, including Gladys! Each year, on their anniversary, Abner would go to the local malt shop and buy an ice cream soda or banana split in memory of the one he and Gladys shared when he proposed. I always felt he should've taken Gladys along!

Vanilla ice cream
Strawberry ice cream
Chocolate ice cream
Bananas (1 per person)
Strawberry topping (Available at markets and ice cream
   shops.)
Chocolate topping   "
Pineapple topping   "
Whipped cream
Chopped walnuts
Maraschino cherries

Per person:

In a long sundae dish, place 1 scoop each of strawberry, vanilla, and chocolate ice cream all in a row. Peel banana and split lengthwise. Place a half along each side of dish.

Pour chocolate topping over strawberry ice cream, pineapple topping over vanilla ice cream, and strawberry topping over chocolate ice cream. Or, mix them any way you wish.

Put dollop of whipped cream on top of each scoop of ice cream. Sprinkle with chopped walnuts and top each dollop with a maraschino cherry.

Yum! But, don't count the calories.

✳ Mrs. Kravitz's Special Vegetarian Feast for Samantha and Darrin ✳

[Episode #140, "Splitsville"]

MENU
Alfalfa Soup

Organic Vegetable Loaf

Abner's Steamed Veggies

Soy Bean Brownies

✳

Note: I suggest you just skip the whole thing and send out for cold cuts and beer as Darrin and Abner wanted to do in Episode #140.

[—K.R.]

Oh, well . . . if you insist . . .

Alfalfa Soup

Generous as Gladys usually is with her health-food philosophy, she steadfastly refused to give us her secret recipe for Alfalfa Soup . . . for which we are eternally grateful.

[—K.R.]

"I regard the human body as a furnace and I regard food as what we stoke it with!"

—Gladys Kravitz

[Episode #140, "Splitsville"]

Abner's Steamed Veggies

While Gladys was away visiting her mother, his sister Harriet would cook this for him. Considering how steamed he always got over Gladys and her "nonsense," Abner always liked it!

Allow 20 to 25 minutes overall.

Place a couple of inches of water in a large pot. Insert holder for vegetables so they are suspended above the water. Bring water to a boil.

Scrub and cut veggies as desired. Any assortment will do and you may steam them all in the same pot. Start with veggies that take the longest to steam.

> **Carrots**
> **Potatoes, halved**
> **Beets**

Steam, covered for about 10 minutes: (Heat may be lowered to medium or medium-high, if desired.)

Add:

> **Whole squash (summer, yellow, zucchini, etc.)**
> **Cauliflower flowerets**
> **Onions, halved**

Steam for another 8–10 minutes.

Add:

> **Broccoli flowerets**
> **Green beans**

Continue steaming until all are *al dente.* Do not overcook.

Season to taste with salt, pepper, butter, a spoonful of mayonnaise, and chunks of Cheddar cheese inserted in squash, or simply sprinkle all with Parmesan or Romano.

Gladys: Proper nutrition is the key to vitality.

[Episode #140, "SPLITSVILLE"]

Soy Bean Brownies

Preheat oven to 350°F.

⅓   c. Unbleached white flour
⅔   c. Water
½   lb. Tofu (Here come da soy beans. Tofu is made from
       them.)

Whisk flour and water until there are no lumps.
Whip tofu until smooth and creamy.
Blend the flour and water mixture and tofu, and stir constantly over low heat until thickened. Cool completely.

To cooled mixture, add:

2   c. Sugar
1   tsp. Salt
1   tsp. Vanilla

Beat well.

In another bowl combine:

¾   c. Cocoa
½   c. Oil

Then, add tofu mixture and mix well.

Mix together:

1½   c. Unbleached white flour
1   scant tsp. Baking powder

Blend all ingredients together. Bake in a well oiled and floured square pan about 25 minutes. Use the old toothpick test for doneness.

More Kravitz Trivia

Abner and Gladys weren't the only neighbors the Stephens had. In the house to the left, a dwelling once owned by TV's first perfect maid, Hazel, lived Danger O'Reilly (Beverly Adams) and her sister Priscilla, better known as "Pleasure" (Kipp Hamilton). And next door to the Kravitzes lived the elderly Miss Parsons (Ruth McDevitt) in a home she later shared with Tony and Jeannie Nelson!

What "First Family of Song" also resided in the Kravitzes' home?
Hint: It wasn't the Brady Bunch!
The Partridge Family.

A true crime that only two actors from Bewitched ever won an Emmy. Can you name them?
Both Alice Pearce and Marion Lorne won the Emmy Award for Outstanding Performance by an Actress in a Supporting Role in a Comedy. Both awards were presented posthumously.

Gladys: How did you enjoy your dinner, Mr. Stephens?
Darrin: Uhhh, it, uhmmm, was highly *original!*

✳   ✳   ✳

Abner: Come on in and have some breakfast. If you like your pancakes rare, you're in luck!
Gladys refuses to turn on the stove, thinking she has the power to will it on.

[Episode #29, "Abner Kadabra"]

✳   ✳   ✳

Gladys: How can you be so calm? Nobody ever had *square green spots* before!
Abner: Nobody ever had your Chicken Soup before!

Gladys Kravitz's Chicken Noodle Soup

An absolute favorite of Gladys' brother Louis: "The Chicken Fiddler"

2½–3	lb. Frying chicken, cut up
10	c. Water
1	c. Onions, finely chopped
1	clove Garlic, minced
	Salt, to taste
	Pepper, to taste
½	tsp. Thyme leaves, crushed
6	Peppercorns (or dash of pepper)
1	c. Celery, thinly sliced
1	c. Carrots, thinly sliced
1	c. Noodles

In large Dutch oven, combine chicken and water and bring to a boil.

Remove surface scum. Reduce heat. Cover and simmer 15 minutes.

Add onions, garlic, salt, pepper, thyme, and peppercorns. Simmer covered 35 to 45 minutes longer.

When chicken is tender, remove chicken and peppercorns from broth.

Cool. Remove chicken from bones. Discard skin. Cut into bite-size pieces.

Skim fat from the broth. Again, bring broth to a boil.

Stir in carrots, celery, and chicken pieces. Reduce heat. Cover and simmer 20 minutes longer. Add noodles and cook for another 10 to 12 minutes.

SERVES 9 TO 10.

"I've nursed over 200 of my friends back to health with my chicken soup. The Mayo Clinic should offer me a consulting position."

—Gladys (Or was that Sandy?)

Samantha: I know you like my banana cake better than Mrs. Kravitz's.

Darrin: At least you peel the bananas!

Gladys Kravitz's New and Improved Banana Cake

Hang a bunch of bananas in garage to ripen. Peel when ready for use.

2	c. All-purpose flour
1½	c. Sugar
1½	tsp. Baking powder
¾	tsp. Baking soda
½	tsp. Salt
½	tsp. Cinnamon
1	c. Ripe bananas, mashed
½	c. Buttermilk
½	c. Shortening
2	large Eggs
1	tsp. Vanilla
½	Tbs. Lemon juice or white vinegar

Combine flour, sugar, baking powder, baking soda, salt, and cinnamon in large bowl. Add bananas, buttermilk, shortening, eggs, and vanilla.

With an electric mixer, beat on low speed till combined. Beat on medium speed for 3 minutes.

Pour batter into 2 greased and floured 8- or 9-inch by 1½-inch, round baking pans.

Bake at 350°F. for 30–35 minutes or till toothpick comes out clean.

Cool on racks for 10 minutes. Remove from pans, cool on racks.

Walnut—Cream Cheese Frosting

2	3-oz. pkg. Cream cheese
½	c. Butter, softened
½	tsp. Cinnamon
2	tsps. Vanilla
4½–5	c. Powdered sugar, sifted
¾	c. Walnuts, chopped finely
1	tsp. Cinnamon
2	tsp. Powdered sugar
1	8-inch or 9-inch paper doily

In large bowl, beat cream cheese, butter, ½ tsp. cinnamon, and vanilla till light and fluffy.

Gradually add 2 cups powdered sugar, beating well.

Gradually beat in only enough remaining powdered sugar to make frosting spread smoothly.

Fold in walnuts.

Frost top of one layer of Banana Cake. Place second layer on top and proceed to frost sides and top.

Chill cake for 30 minutes.

Place paper doily lightly on cake.

Mix 1 teaspoon cinnamon and 2 teaspoons powdered sugar. Dust over doily allowing mixture to fall into pattern on top of cake.

What isn't devoured can be stored in the fridge under cover.

✳ Gladys' "Medicine" ✳

After years of secrecy, we found out that Gladys' medicine was really Abner's own "happy" concoction.

    1   **Spoon (preferably a tablespoon)**
    1   **Empty bottle**
         Benedictine
         Brandy

Fill bottle halfway with Benedictine, rest of the way with brandy.

Blend.

In case of emergency, administer 1 spoonful at a time.

Abner assures us that any resemblance to a "B & B" is purely coincidental.

The "Endorable" In-Laws

ENDORA AND MAURICE

Endora

The volatile, flamboyant, and sometimes vindictive Endora was born long before the turn of the century (vanity prevents her from telling which one)! The earliest known reference to her is a written account of King Saul's journeys seeking a spell to raise the dead!

Once compared to the Wicked Witch of the West, she indignantly exclaimed: "I refuse to stay here another minute and be compared to an amateur!"

In a time when people still wore armor, Endora was swept off her feet by the suave and debonair Maurice. They married and within a century, Endora gave birth to her only child Samantha on the eve of the "Galactic Rejuvenation and Dinner Dance."

Although they have never actually undergone an Ectoplasmic Interlocutory (the witches' version of Divorce Court!), Endora threatens Maurice with it on several occasions.

Endora has since had brief romantic flings with the likes of Sir Walter Raleigh and other historic notables. Her one mortal affair, with a client of Darrin's named Bo Callahan, was strictly due to an errant love potion that went awry.

Always opposed to her daughter's mixed marriage, Endora nonetheless delights in her two absolutely "Endorable" grandchildren.

✳ Endora's *New* Dinner Menu ✳

Louise: Any good cook can make Lobster Thermidor!
Endora: Out of Pot Roast?!

[Episode #198, "MONA SAMMY"]

MENU

Endora's Lobster Thermidor

Courteous Cream Sauce

Steamed Rice

Wishful Asparagus Spears

Salad Sorcery

Autumn Flame Salad Dressing

Endora's Wrath

Endora's Lobster Thermidor

Start with Samantha's Pot Roast found on page 8. Discard.

1 lb. Lobster meat, cubed
1 c. Fresh mushrooms, sliced (or canned)
4 tsps. Parsley, chopped

2 tsps. Paprika
1 tsp. Dry mustard
½ tsp. Salt
  Pepper, to taste
½ Lemon, juiced
3–4 Tbs. Butter, melted
3 c. Cream sauce, medium thick (Recipe follows.)
¼ c. Sherry
4 Eggs, hard boiled and diced (optional)
4 Tbsp. Parmesan cheese

Combine lobster, mushrooms, parsley, paprika, mustard, salt, pepper, and lemon juice. Sauté in melted butter. Remove from heat.

Prepare Cream Sauce. Add Cream Sauce, sherry, and eggs (if desired). Combine lobster and Cream Sauce mixtures. Spoon into large casserole. Sprinkle with Parmesan cheese.

Bake in moderate (325–350°F.) oven 10 to 12 minutes or until bubbly and brown.

Serve at once over steamed rice as prepared according to directions on package.

SERVES 6 TO 8.

One of the earliest known photographs of Endora. Before this we have tintypes, oil paintings, and hieroglyphics!

COURTESY AGNES MOOREHEAD PRIVATE COLLECTION

"Courteous, chivalrous, gallant is he?
Well, if he isn't now, he soon will be!
With a root of Hemlock and a sting of bee,
I shall give him instant courtesy!"

Endora, Queen of the Nasties, does her thing!

[Episode #153, "INSTANT COURTESY"]

Courteous Cream Sauce

Courteous Cream Sauce is the perfect complement to Endora's Lobster Thermidor. It is also known as your basic White Sauce, or Béchamel.

> 3   c. Milk, heated
> 4   Tbsp. Butter
> 4   Tbsp. Flour
>   Salt, to taste
>   Pepper, to taste (Fresh ground is always best.)

Warm milk, but do not boil. Melt butter in heavy skillet or saucepan.

Slowly stir flour into melted butter. Continue stirring a minute or two until the paste bubbles and cooks. Do not brown!

Slowly add hot milk, stirring all the while. As you bring to a boil, the sauce will thicken.

Add salt and pepper to taste.

Lower heat and continue cooking another minute or two. Sauce should be smooth and light in texture.

✳   ✳   ✳

Bewitched, Bothered, and Bejeweled: Irene Vernon had this fond memory of Agnes Moorehead: "Agnes used to wear a lot of her own magnificent jewlery on *Bewitched*. But not all pieces were used in a scene. Agnes would let me, as Louise, wear her "spare" jewlery so it wouldn't be left behind, unguarded, in her dressing room.

Speaking of Agnes' dressing room, Kasey recalls it well: "Agnes

Samantha: Well, do you
want to stay for dinner?
Endora: What are we
eating? Crow?

Endora gloats at Samantha
who worries that Darrin
has used three wishes to
get snowed in with a
beautiful campaign model.

[Episode #96, "THREE
WISHES"]

Moorehead's dressing room was the most lavish of all! Instead of the simple dressing table and cot, hers was fully furnished, decorated in lavenders and purples, replete with gilt tables and ornate beaded lamps."

* * *

Wishful Asparagus Spears

Wash and remove 1 inch of lower stems if necessary. Then, simply steam until tender (not limp).

If accompanying Lobster Thermidor, serve with lemon wedges only.

Salad Sorcery

1   head Bibb lettuce
1   medium Onion, cut into rings
1   8-oz. can Mandarin orange slices
1   small jar Pine nuts

Wash, dry and tear lettuce. (Crisp in fridge until serving time.)
Transfer to salad bowl or individual plates.
Cut and separate onion rings. Arrange over lettuce.
Drain mandarin oranges and arrange over lettuce.
Sprinkle with pine nuts.
Add salad dressing and serve.

Autumn Flame Salad Dressing

Ahhh, memories of an evening when Endora herself almost
married a mortal! Her Autumn Flame Salad Dressing, a potent
love potion, was named after Bo Callahan (Arch Johnson) and
his Autumn Flame Perfume, which gave Endora an evening she
would never live down . . . er . . . forget.

[Episode #125, "Once in a Vial"]

½   c. Extra virgin olive oil
4   Tbs. Light vinegar (Tarragon is great.)
1   tsp. Salt
     Pepper, to taste, freshly ground
½   clove Garlic

Mix all in container with lid and shake well. Refrigerate until
serving time. Remove garlic clove and shake again. (Do not leave
garlic clove in dressing.)
To vary taste, add a few drops of onion juice or Tabasco or

Worchestershire. Try a few dashes of dry mustard or curry powder.

To thicken, add a dollop of mayonnaise and shake well before serving.

Christmas, Endora Style: Agnes Moorehead delighted in throwing the first Christmas party of the season on her birthday, December 6th. Her lovely Beverly Hills home was crowded with Hollywood's elite, including Lucille Ball and Debbie Reynolds, as well as the *Bewitched* cast. Agnes served her sit-down dinner on her large back patio at tables seating six or eight. Wine was served in colored glasses, each shaped like a cluster of grapes.

[—K.R.]

Endora's Wrath

       Vanilla ice cream
1   c. Peach, apricot, or strawberry preserves
1   c. Coconut, shredded
3–4 jiggers Puerto Rican rum (Spiced is nice.)

Heat preserves and coconut in a lovely chafing dish until hot.

Place one scoop of ice cream per person in stemmed crystal goblets. (Actually, any dessert dish is O.K.)

Add rum to preserves and mix gently.

Endora now ignites this mixture with a scathing glance. You, however, may have to use a match.

Carefully spoon the flaming preserves over each portion of ice cream and serve with dainty cookie.

Lavender Illusions: Agnes was as flamboyant in real life as she was on-screen, recalls Kasey. Of life and acting, with a flourish of her arms, she would say, "I love the illusion!"

Also known as "The Lavender Lady," Agnes insisted that she be surrounded by her favorite color, lavender. This included not only her dressing room at the studio, but her house, its furnishings, and even her car.

✳ Endora's Cosmic " 'Twas the Night Before Halloween" Party ✳

Endora: 'Twas the Night Before Halloween . . .
                And all who were chic,
                Were sipping champagne . . .
Uncle Arthur: They'd been stoned for a week!

(Endora starts to get irritated . . .)

Endora: The Witches and Warlocks . . .
                In Rome by the score,
                With their ladies attired in their best, by Dior . . .
Uncle Arthur: Checking their warts as they came through the door!

(Now, she's steamed!)

Endora: And, the odd little mortals, all snug in their beds,
                While visions of Trick-or-Treats danced in their heads.
                Our children were practicing their spells and their chants—
Uncle Arthur: And even the Poltergeists pulled off their pants!

(At this point, Endora turns him into a fountain!)

[Episode #81, "TWITCH OR TREAT"]

MENU
Boris and Ava's Favorite Champagne

Black Beluga Cavier

Sea Urchins with Bordelaise Sauce (Stuft Mushrooms)

Boiled Ostrich with Sweet and Sour Sauce (Sweet and Sour Meatballs)

Turtle Doves Sautéed in Feathers (Potato Skins)

Roast Parrot and Dormice Stuffed with Porcupine Kernels (Chicken Divine . . . or Is That Divan)

"I see Boris has brought his 'Ghoul Friend!' "

[Arthur in Episode #81, "Twitch or Treat"]

Boris and Ava's Favorite Champagne

The only champagne Endora would think of serving is Dom Perignon.

'Tis rumored when Dom Perignon first perfected his heavenly libation, Endora complimented him with "It's like drinking stars."

Or was it Dom Perignon who said that?

Black Beluga Caviar

Expensive and elegant.

The classic way of serving black caviar is to accompany it with:

Hard-boiled egg whites, finely chopped
Hard-boiled egg yolks, finely chopped
Onions, finely minced
Lemon wedges
Thin strips of dry, unbuttered toast or toasted rounds

Serve your black caviar in a crystal (or otherwise pretty) bowl and set it in a bed of crushed ice.

On another lovely serving dish, or in individual bowls, serve the egg whites, egg yolks, onion, lemon, and toast.

ENDORA'S "TRICKS-OR-TREATS" CANAPÉS

Note: Many of the ingredients Endora enjoys such as ostrich, sea urchins, and porcupine kernels are scarce in the mortal world. But we decided to name our canapés after hers anyway.

Endora (disguised as a little girl): "Miztle-Picket-Razza-Ta-Mick!"
   You've been tricked! You better watch out!
Darrin: I'm not worried, I've been tricked by experts!

Darrin, not realizing it's Endora, doesn't know he's about to be changed into a werewolf!

[Episode #43, "TRICK-OR-TREAT"]

Sea Urchins with Bordelaise Sauce (Stuft Mushrooms)

20   Large, perfect mushrooms.

Wash and dry mushrooms. Remove stems and set aside.

8   Tbs. Butter
½   c. Bread crumbs (or more)
¼   c. Green onions, chopped
1   clove Garlic, minced
1   Tbs. Parsley, chopped
1   Egg, lightly beaten (optional)
½   c. Freshly grated Parmesan, Cheddar, or blue cheese

   Salt, to taste
   Pepper, to taste
1 **Box toothpicks**

   Melt ½ butter and let cool. Coat mushroom caps, top and bottom, with melted butter. Place in baking dish.
   Chop stems (about 1 cupful). Combine with all ingredients except butter. Mix well. Fill each mushroom cap. Melt the balance of the butter and drizzle over each filled cap. Dust with Parmesan.
   Preheat oven to 350°F. Bake for 15 to 20 minutes.
   To make canapés look more like sea urchins, stick several toothpicks randomly thru mushrooms and place on platter.

Other Goblin Mushroom Stuffings

"Goblins and Gremlins, when I look,
You'll be off the street and back in the book!"

Samantha tries to save the neighborhood from Tabatha's "friends"!

[Episode #115, "THE SAFE AND SANE HALLOWEEN"]

Spooky Spinach Stuffing

   Prepare as for sea urchins, except replace cheese with 1 cup of cooked, fresh, well-drained spinach, ¼ cup grated Parmesan, and a little dried marjoram.

Scary Sausage Stuffing

   Or, prepare as previously outlined, except reduce bread crumbs to ¼ cup and leave out the butter and cheese. Sauté ½ pound of sausage (Italian is good) with stem mixture until sausage is browned. Drain well. Add 2 to 4 tablespoons grated Parmesan and bread crumbs, and stuff mushrooms.
   Bake as above.

Boiled Ostrich with Sweet and Sour Sauce (Sweet & Sour Meatballs)

1   c. Bread crumbs
2   lbs. Ground chuck
¼   c. Onions, chopped
1   clove Garlic, crushed
1   tsp. Salt
⅛   tsp. Cayenne pepper
1   c. Milk
¼   tsp. Pepper, black
    Cooking oil

Soften bread crumbs in the milk. Mix all ingredients except cooking oil. Form into meatballs.

Heat cooking oil in heavy skillet. Sauté meatballs in oil. Set aside to drain.

SERVES 8.

Sauce

1   c. Pineapple, crushed
1   c. Green pepper, finely chopped
½   c. Vinegar
¼   c. Brown sugar
¾   c. Water
1   Tbs. Molasses
1   Tbs. Cornstarch

Mix all of the sauce ingredients. If too thick, add a little pineapple juice or water.

Place drained meatballs in casserole. Cover with sauce. Bake at 325°F. for 30 minutes.

"If mother wanted to spoil the party, it would be raining in the living room!"

Samantha to Darrin on their anniversary.

[Episode #76, "THE MOMENT OF TRUTH"]

Turtle Doves Sautéed in Feathers (Potato Skins)

6   small Potatoes

Grease outside of potatoes and bake at 350°F. for 30 to 40 minutes or until done.

Slice in half lengthwise. Scoop out center leaving ¼-inch shell. Place shells on cookie sheet. (Optional: May bake shells an additional 10 minutes if you want them to be crisp.)

1½   c. Cheddar cheese, grated
½   c. Green onions, chopped
½   c. Bacon, fried crisp and crumbled into small pieces
Salsa (optional)

Mix Cheddar cheese, chopped green onions, and bacon bits well.

Fill potato shells with mixture and broil for 10 minutes or until cheese is bubbling and shells warmed.

Serve with Salsa on the side.

Haunted Halloween Main Course

Larry: If it isn't the glamorous, ever-popular Endora.
Endora: A simple curtsy will do!

At least one mortal knew how to properly greet a powerful Witch like Endora.

[Episode #198, "MONA SAMMY"]

Roast Parrot and Dormice Stuffed with Porcupine Kernels

(Chicken Divine . . . or, is that Divan)

2 large Parrots
2 large Dormice

Since it is illegal to roast parrots and too hard to catch dormice, you may substitute:

4 large Chicken breasts, skinned

Continue with:

¾ tsp. Salt
1 large pkg. Broccoli, frozen spears
1 c. Cream of chicken soup
½ c. Sour cream
½ c. Mayonnaise
1 tsp. Paprika
3–4 Tbs. Dry sherry (optional)
1 tsp. Mustard
¼ tsp. Curry powder
½ c. Parmesan cheese, grated
½ c. Cheddar cheese, grated
1 7-oz. can Mushrooms, drained

In large Dutch oven, cover chicken breasts with water. Add salt and boil until chicken is easily pulled from bones (about 1 hour). Remove chicken and cool. Chop chicken and set aside.

Prepare broccoli according to package directions. Drain and place in long buttered casserole dish placing the flowerets facing the sides of dish.

Add chopped chicken pieces over broccoli. Combine all other ingredients and pour over chicken and broccoli. Bake 350°F. for

25 minutes. Sprinkle with additional cheese and paprika. Bake
for an additional 5 minutes until top cheese is melted.
Serve over Naked Wild Rice.
SERVES 4 TO 6.

Naked Wild Rice:

Special occasion treat. Distinctive nutlike flavor and texture.
Best prepared as simply as possible.

> **3 c. Water**
> **1 c. Wild rice**
> **Salt, to taste**
> **Butter**

Rinse rice very well. Add salt to water and bring to a boil.
Slowly add the rice. Reduce heat and simmer for 45 minutes or
more, until rice has absorbed all the water and is tender. Stir in
butter, toss, and serve.
YIELDS 3 CUPS.

Gladys: I tell you, she turned my nephew into a goat! Right in
the kitchen! And he won't come out! Oh, what'll I tell my sister?!

[Episode #115, "THE SAFE AND SANE HALLOWEEN"]

"That was the most unusual Halloween Party I'd ever been to.
It sure beats dunking for apples!"

Darrin to Samantha as he happily recovers from Halloween of
1966.

[Episode #81, "TWITCH OR TREAT"]

✳ ✳ ✳

Agnes of God. During and after *Bewitched,* Agnes used to teach acting at her own school. Bernard Fox, who sometimes taught for her,
recalls that she would hold church services in her home on Sundays
for all her staff and students, with the "Reverend Endora" presiding!

✳ ✳ ✳

Mother Trivia

What is the name of the car Endora zaps up for Darrin in Episode #93, "Super Car"?
The Reactor Mach II

Not only did Agnes Moorehead play Samantha's mother, she was "mom" to other famous stars as well. Name two.
Kathryn Grayson's mother in *Showboat* and Orson Welles' mom in *Citizen Kane*. Incidentally, *Citizen Kane* was Agnes' first film.

Rarely able to get his name right, what were some of the monikers Endora tagged Darrin with?
Durwood, Darwood, Durweed, Dagwood, Darius, Darwin, Dumbo, Dennis, Derick, Dumpkin, Donald, Dum-Dum. Sorry, "Dolphin" and "Duspin" were the nicknames Maurice used.

What animated feature was Agnes Moorehead's last work? And what part did she play?
Charlotte's Web. She played the Goose. Paul Lynde was also featured as Templeton, the rat!

Endora's Magical Breakfast Popcorn

This is the same Magic Popcorn that made Darrin, the Milkman, the TV Repairman, Larry, the Client, Mr. Parkinson (Irwin Charone), and even the Cop on the beat forget his daily toils and life's little troubles!

[Episode #85, "OEDIPUS HEX"]

1   c. Light corn syrup
¾   Tbs. Cider vinegar
¼   tsp. Salt
1   tsp. Flavoring (vanilla, peppermint, cherry, wintergreen, your choice)

Few drops Food coloring (yellow, red, green, your choice)
1½ qt. Popped corn, no seasoning
½ c. Walnuts or pecans

Cook corn syrup, vinegar, and salt in heavy pot over medium heat. Stir until it reaches the hard-ball stage (250°F).

Remove from heat. Add flavoring and food coloring. (Use yellow coloring with vanilla flavoring, red coloring with peppermint or cherry flavor, green flavoring with wintergreen, etc.)

Pour popped corn and nuts into large greased bowl. In thin stream, pour syrup over popcorn and nuts, tossing lightly with large, buttered fork

When cool enough to handle, butter hands of all Little Kitchen Witches and let them roll mixture into small balls, crescent moons, or funny shapes. Roll a magical good wish into each individual piece.

Cool on wax paper until no longer sticky.

These treats will magically disappear. If any are left, place in plastic wrap and store at room temperature.

Maurice

The Shakespeare-quoting Maurice is a Renaissance Warlock of great ability, although he has yet to remember his son-in-law's name!

Maurice and Endora hold the distinct title of television's first legally separated couple, as well as its longest married couple, considering their advanced ages! A fact Maurice is justly proud of.

In recent years, he has returned to the Shakespearean stage to portray Macbeth for the seventy-fifth time since it was written for him. Bertha, Hagatha and Enchantra co-starred with him as the Three Witches.

COLUMBIA/SONY SIGNATURE COURTESY
HERBIE J. PILATO

Maurice was quoted as saying to the British press: "It didn't take much acting on their part!"

✳ Maurice's Favorites ✳

"After a century or two I might get to like you as much as I like this champagne. Too bad you won't be around that long!"

Maurice upon first meeting Darrin.

[Episode #10, "JUST ONE HAPPY FAMILY"]

Daddy's Breton Lamb Hot Pot

Maurice Evans loved to putter in the kitchen. The following recipe, contributed by his close friends Mr. and Mrs. Averil Koch, was one of his favorites.

    8   oz. Uncle Ben's Rice
    1   pt. Meat sauce for spaghetti
    1   Onion, sliced
    1   clove Garlic, chopped
    ½   Green pepper, chopped
    4   Lamb chops, trimmed of any fat (one per person)
    1   14-oz. can Tomatoes
        Salt, to taste
        Pepper, to taste
    1   Bay leaf
    1   glass Wine (He didn't say how big a glass!)
        Parsley, chopped (for garnish)

Place rice in large casserole. Pour meat sauce over rice.
Add onion, garlic, and green pepper.
Arrange lamb chops on top. Season well and add bay leaf.
Pour canned tomatoes over all. (Reserve some tomato juice to add later.)
Bake at 350°F. for 1 hour.
Add wine and extra tomato juice, as needed. Continue bak-

COURTESY OF THE AVERIL KOCH COLLECTION

 "This is my favorite picture of Maurice. Relaxed, happy, playing the piano and singing. His favorite pastime."

ing for an additional ½ to 1 hour. (Overall baking time 1½ to 2 hours.)

Garnish and serve.

And, as Maurice always concluded his recipes, *"Bon Appétit."*

SERVES 4.

Maurice: "Samantha, I have not taken away the cause of your happiness, I simply changed his form . . . and not much at that!"

Maurice upon turning Darrin into a jackass.

[Episode #167, "DADDY DOES HIS THING"]

Maurice's Trivia

Who was the rather comely Witch Maurice hired as a private secretary?
Miss Abigail Beechum (Janine Gray). Episode #168, "SAMANTHA'S GOOD NEWS"

Endora and Samantha engage the help of one of Maurice's old nemeses to make him jealous. What was his name and what title did he hold?
The very Australian John Van Millwood (Murray Matheson) who claimed to be "Mr. Torso of Tasmania"!

[Episode #168, "SAMANTHA'S GOOD NEWS"

In what play did Maurice and John Van Millwood appear together and where?
Julius Caesar in Brisbane, Australia. The Annual Warlocks' Coven

Maurice: You were Brutus to my Anthony! An interpretation calculated to cause the stones of Rome to rise and mutiny!

[Episode #168, "SAMANTHA'S GOOD NEWS"]

In 1968 Maurice made a monkey (without a spell) out of himself in this feature film.
Planet of the Apes. Look closely he's the only blond ape!

Maurice Evans appeared in what movie about possession? Hint: It was about a bad baby and also starred one of Kasey's Peyton Place co-stars.
Rosemary's Baby. A film that both Endora and Uncle Arthur protest against in *Bewitched!*

✳ ✳ ✳

Moniker Magic! In Episode #168, "Samantha's Good News," John Van Millwood (Murray Matheson) pronounced Maurice as "Morris." He was hotly corrected. In truth, Maurice Evans pronounced his own name "Morris."

✳ ✳ ✳

Pop Goes The Dishes! Maurice was forever breaking china lamps and other crockery about Samantha's living room when he was exceptionally angry. To accomplish this feat of magic the special effects department would either detonate a small explosive charge inside the prop or an off-camera sharpshooter would aim a rifle and blow it away with a pellet!

In his first episode, #10, "Just One Happy Family," it made him very nervous, and he can be seen to jump each time it happens. By Episode #176, however, Warlock Maurice was an old pro and didn't so much as flinch!

✳ ✳ ✳

Phyllis: Wh-wh-what was that all about?
Darrin: About a hundred and fifty dollars the way I figure it!

[Episode #176, "Naming Samantha's New Baby"]

Maurice's "Crackin' Crockery" Curried Eggs

"Grandpapa" Maurice loved curry. Here it is for breakfast.

2–3	Tbs. Butter
1	c. Onions, chopped

Melt butter and sauté onions lightly. In separate bowl, combine:

> 6 **Eggs**
> ¼–½ **c. Milk**
> 2–3 **Tbs. Curry**

Beat together. When blended, add to sautéed onions and scramble.
SERVES 2.
"Bon Appétit," Maurice Evans.

Endora: You bring him back or I'll make your life miserable for you, and you know I can do it! I'll move in with you!

Endora to Maurice, after he vaporized Darrin.

[Episode #10, "JUST ONE HAPPY FAMILY"]

Endora and Maurice's Very Dry Martini

"Daddy Does His Thing," Episode #167
"Mother Meets What's-His-Name," Episode #4
2½ **oz. Spanish gin**
   Dash Italian vermouth
1 **Greek olive**

Darrin never seemed to have the appropriate ingredients on hand.

"Don't bother, I'll make it myself!" Endora or Maurice would snap and materialize their own.

"My wife and I have what might be described as an informal marriage."

[Maurice in Episode #168, "SAMANTHA'S GOOD NEWS"]

PHYLLIS AND FRANK STEPHENS

Frank and Phyllis Stephens

Frank Stephens proposed to Phyllis Barrington during a thunderstorm at Angel Falls, New York. They were married on Nov. 2, 1932. Phyllis always kept the green scarf she was wearing. Unaware of their daughter-in-law's adeptness at sorcery, Phyllis thinks the only oddity in the family is her own sister Madge, who believes she's a lighthouse! "Every time it rains she climbs onto the garage roof to warn the sailors!" Darrin told Samantha on their wedding night.

Originally hailing from Missouri, Frank and Phyllis moved closer to Darrin and Samantha after the birth of their first grandchild, Tabatha. This mainly served to increase Phyllis' propensity to sick headaches.

Many readers will be interested to know that Phyllis' Mynah bird, Black Bart, lived to a ripe old age and never actually suffered from a sick headache!

✳ Phyllis' Sick Headache Recipes ✳

"Frank, I've got a sick headache!"

[Phyllis Stephens (Mabel Albertson) in numerous *Bewitched* episodes.]

Warlock Tea from Episode #91, "Sam in the Moon"

A special blend of herbs and spices that Endora got from a Japanese Warlock herbalist. Darrin, thinking it to be Moon Dust, had it analyzed at Grand's Drug Store.

The Spicy Chai recipe below is the result of the apothecary's analysis.

Note: This same tea was prepared by Lord Ocky (Reginald Owen) to cure one of Mrs. Stephens' sick headaches in Episode #130, "McTavish." Mrs. Stephens insisted on the recipe and, now having used it so often, thinks she originated it.

Phyllis' Sick Headache Spicy Chai Tea

32	oz. Water
1½	in. Fresh ginger root
3	pods Cardamom
4	Cloves
3	Tbs. Black tea
16	oz. Milk
2	Tbs. Sugar

In a large pot, bring water to a boil.

Slice the ginger root into ¼-inch slices cutting long way. Lay the cut ginger on one side of a paper towel and fold the other side over the slices. *Lightly* pound the ginger with a mallet to release the juices then add to boiling pot of water.

Crush the cardamom seeds. Add cardamom and cloves to water.

Let the spices simmer for at least 20 minutes. (For optimum strength, allow the ginger and spices to soak overnight in the water.)

After 20 minutes, add the black tea to the pot and bring to a brisk boil.

Add the milk to the pot and bring to a boil once again. When the Chai begins to bubble up to the top of the pot, then, using a mitt or hot pad, lift the pot off the heat and allow the hot milk to settle down. Place pot on heat again and allow to bubble up to the top of the pot again.

Remove from heat and allow to settle again. Do this 3 times. (This repetition may be more ritualistic than scientific.)

Now add the sugar and bring to a boil one last time. Strain and you are ready to serve. Careful, it's hot!

Note: In India, the spices used for this Chai are traditionally used only when one is not feeling their best. However, it is so delicious that Dr. Bombay prescribes it for any time the craving strikes.

"Zolda, Pranken, Kopek, Lum!"

Hagatha's (Reta Shaw) spell for pouring tea.

[Episode #7, "THE WITCHES ARE OUT"]

Phyllis' Black Bart Sponge Cake

When Black Bart would get on Phyllis' nerves, which was constantly, she would sing about "Four and twenty blackbirds baked in a pie." Phyllis couldn't bring herself to really do it, so she named her best sponge cake after the mimicking fowl.

Parental Trivia

Following a Bewitched trend, can you name the two "Roberts" who portrayed Frank Stephens?
Robert F. Simon and Roy Roberts.

Name the Mynah bird Phyllis bought for Tabatha to play with.
Black Bart.

Did you know that Mabel Albertson did the voice for Black Bart?

Where did Frank ask Phyllis to marry him?
Angel Falls.

6   oz. Semisweet chocolate
4   Eggs
¾   c. Sugar
1   Tbs. Irish Cream Liqueur (optional, may substitute
     vanilla)
1   Tbs. Grated orange peel
     Dash Salt
½   c. Cake flour

Preheat oven to 350°F. Cut wax paper to fit bottom of 9-inch tube pan and line bottom. In top of double boiler, melt the chocolate, then set aside to cool.

Beat the eggs until light and *gradually* add the sugar, Irish Cream, orange peel, and salt. Stir in the melted chocolate. Sift the flour over the batter.

Fold in until just blended. Spoon into pan and bake 40 to 50 minutes.

Test by inserting a straw. When it comes out clean, the cake is done.

✳ Samantha has some double mother trouble on her hands in this still from Episode #19, "A NICE LITTLE DINNER PARTY."

Invert pan on rack and cook cake completely. Remove from pan.

Basic Black Bart Butter Frosting

>   4   Tbs. Butter
>   ¼   c. Cream
>   2   Tbs. Irish Cream Liqueur (or vanilla)
>   3   c. Confectioner's sugar

Cream together the butter, cream, and Irish Cream (or vanilla). Slowly beat in the sugar until thick and creamy. Frost Phyllis' Black Bart Sponge Cake and . . . yum.

Phyllis: Now that we're all here, I have an idea.
Endora: Oh. Beginner's luck!

Pass the kitty some milk! Endora sharpens her claws on Mrs. Stephens in Episode #163, "TABATHA'S WEEKEND."

Phyllis: Can she [Samantha] make chicken cacciatore?
Darrin: No, Mom. No one can make chicken cacciatore the way you can.

[Episode #14, "SAMANTHA MEETS THE FOLKS"]

Phyllis' Chicken Cacciatore

1	medium Chicken (cut in 8 pieces)
¼	c. Olive oil
½	c. Sliced mushrooms, fresh
1	large Onion, chopped
½	c. Dry white wine
1	clove Garlic, minced
1–2	Tbs. Tomato paste
2	c. Fresh tomatoes, peeled, seeded, and chopped (May substitute 1 large can drained tomatoes.)
½	c. Orange juice
2	Bay leaves
1	Tbs. Oregano, crumbled
½	tsp. Thyme
	Salt, to taste
	Freshly ground pepper, to taste
1	tsp. Lemon zest
	Parsley, finely chopped

Heat the oil in a heavy skillet and lightly brown chicken on all sides. Add the mushrooms and onions, sauté a couple of minutes, then pour in the wine and let it boil up. Lower heat and add garlic, tomato paste, tomatoes, orange juice, and seasoning. Cover and it's slow cookin' for about 40 minutes, or until ten-

der. Remove bay leaves. Adjust seasoning. Sprinkle parsley and lemon zest over top.
   SERVES 4 TO 5.

Phyllis: You cured his rash?
Samantha: Oh, yes. We found out he only got it when he ate chicken cacciatore.

[Episode #14, "S<small>AMANTHA</small> M<small>EETS THE</small> F<small>OLKS</small>"]

Maurice: Tell me something, Frank. Uhh, by the way, is that short for Franklin?
Frank: No, just plain Frank.
Maurice: Ah, an appellation you must share with the lowly hot dog! Still it's a good, simple, unadorned name.
Frank: Yeah, well, it suits me.
Maurice: Down to the ground!

Darrin's father (Roy Roberts this time) and Maurice discuss the "Importance of Being Frank."

[Episode #176, "N<small>AMING</small> S<small>AMANTHA'S</small> N<small>EW</small> B<small>ABY</small>"]

✳ **Frank's Lowly Franks and Salad** ✳

Frank's Lowly Franks

   Frank, like many husbands of that era, was totally helpless in the kitchen. It took years before Phyllis solved the problem by buying a microwave and teaching him this surefire survival trick to be used in her absence.

1   Hot dog
1   Hot dog bun
1   Paper napkin

Place hot dog inside hot dog bun. Open paper napkin. Roll hot dog inside bun up in the paper napkin.

Microwave for 1 minute only.

Unwrap carefully. (It'll be hot!) Spread mustard or mayo or whatever and enjoy.

If still hungry, repeat procedure.

Simon's Savory Salad

Robert L. Simon, son of Robert F. contributed the following so we could include a recipe from "Darrin's dad." "He made it every day for as long as I can remember!"

1 wooden salad bowl (No other will do, the bigger the better.)
1 clove of garlic, sliced thin.

Add garlic to bowl. Smash the garlic around the bottom of the bowl with a wooden spoon until well pulverized (no chunks).

Quantities are up to you.

Add to bowl:

2–3   Scallions, sliced
      Celery, finely sliced
      Carrots, sliced or shredded
      Green bell pepper, chopped
      Lettuce, torn Romaine, iceberg, or both
      Spice Island Salad Seasoning (orange in color) (Shake
         a couple of times.)

Add:

      Salt and pepper
      Red wine vinegar and oil, to taste

Mix well for at least 3 minutes to ensure the garlic blends.

Mother Goose: Would you like to come out to the garden with me
   while I feed Miss Muffet her curds and whey?
Frank: I wouldn't miss it!

As soon as she found out her stories were in print, Mother Goose
(Jane Connell) insisted on being called The "World's Foremost
Writer of Children's Fiction." But, she wasn't above flirting with
Frank (Roy Roberts).

[Episode #182, "SAMANTHA'S DOUBLE MOTHER TROUBLE"]

Serena's "I Hate to Cook" Quickies

Serena

Samantha's cousin on her father's side, Serena has been a frustrated rock star since the early 60's!

Serena did, however, receive some recognition with her recording of "The Iffin Song," a tune made famous by The Belters on the flip side of "America the Beautiful." After she was out of earshot, Louise Tate was heard to say "The Iffin Song" was one of the worst things she'd ever had to sit through!

One thing can be said for Serena, she keeps up with the times. In the early part of this century she was a suffragette, picketing for women's rights and by 1919 had single-handedly started the entire flapper phenomenon. Serena was wearing pants before World War One and by the 1960's had "freaked out" with the flower children.

The first to wear sexy lingerie onstage, Serena is currently suing Pop singer Madonna for impersonating her.

Kick-a-Poo Joy Juice

In another vain attempt to get Samantha away from Darrin, Endora zaps a "Corsican Brothers" spell on her and Serena, so everything Serena feels, Samantha will too! That way Samantha could feel what she was missing in the wonderful world of Witches! Serena, however, only got smashed so Endora zapped the drink away from her!

[Episode #211, "THE CORSICAN COUSINS"]

> 2   oz. Bourbon or rye
> 1   lump Sugar
>   Sprig Fresh mint

Set silver mint julep cup on saucer. (A tall glass will do in a pinch.)

Set in freezer to allow frost to form.

To serve, put sprig of mint, sugar cube, and a teaspoon of bourbon or rye in the bottom of the cup and crush with spoon. Fill cup with finely shaved ice and tamp down firmly.

Add ½ of whiskey and stir gently, not to bruise.

Continue adding ice and whiskey until glass is full of ice and hard packed.

Add a sprig of mint and a warm summer day.

Caution: Broomless flying strictly prohibited.

✳   ✳   ✳

Now, THAT'S funny: Episode #128, "Hippie, Hippie Hooray" is the only episode in which no laugh track was used. A laugh track is pre-recorded laughter that is used in a sitcom to simulate a live studio audience. *Bewitched* was not a live show due to the special effects it employed.

✳   ✳   ✳

Serena's Flower-Power Preserved Flowers

We all know Serena hates to cook, however, she will go to great lengths to always have preserved violets, roses, and other edible flowers on hand.

She's been known to dance the night away in order to be awake to pick fresh flowers at the crack of dawn.

Her little "preserves" will garnish cakes, fruit salads, and tea plates, or be nibbled from a lovely cut-glass compote.

Stored in fancy glass jars, they make unique Christmas Gifts.

1   c. Hot water
2   c. Granulated sugar
4   c. Fresh stemmed violets, washed and drained (Do not bruise petals.)
   If roses are used, measure 2 cups fresh small buds, washed, drained, stemmed.

Dissolve the sugar thoroughly in the hot water. Add the flowers, set on medium heat, and let syrup simmer until it reaches the soft-ball stage in cold water.

Stir flowers gently with wooden spoon. Remove from flame and continue to stir until the syrup begins to granulate and reaches the consistency of coarse meal.

Empty over a wire rack or colander, and shake off the extra sugar. Cool and pack into jars. Seal.

These will keep indefinitely.

Whether blond or brunet, Serena keeps the pot boiling.

Fast And Fudgy Vitamin V Cake

¼ lb. Butter, melted
2 squares Baking chocolate, melted
4 Eggs
2 c. Sugar
1 c. Flour
1 tsp. Vanilla
1 c. Walnuts, chopped

Combine all ingredients mixing only until smooth. Pour into greased baking pan 9 by 9 by 2 inches.

Trivia à la Serena

Usually the dark-haired vixen, Serena did actually appear as a blonde in some episodes. Which ones?
   Episode #111, "Double, Double, Toil and Trouble" and #128, "Hippie, Hippie Hooray"

What former MGM star and Kennedy in-law once dated Serena in an episode?
   Peter Lawford as Harrison Woolcott in Episode #245, "Serena's Richcraft"

Many people feel that Serena was actually played by Elizabeth Montgomery. While this may be true, what name was in the closing credits?
   "Pandora Spocks." Melody Johnson, Elizabeth's stand-in, however, deserves much of the credit for making Serena "credible"!

Bake in preheated 350° F. oven for approximately 45 minutes (until toothpick inserted in middle comes out clean). Cool 15 minutes.

Cut into large squares and duck the choc-o-holics who will smell this a mile away.

"The Iffin Song"

Iffin, Iffin, Iffin, Iffin . . .
Iffin you wanna feel my embrace,
Don't you ever wash your face!
Iffin you wanna leave me weak and weepy,
Ya gotta look wild and weird and creepy!
Iffin, Iffin, Iffin, Iffin . . . Yeah! Yeah! Yeah!

   —As warbled by Serena.

   [Episode #128, "Hippie, Hippie Hooray"]

"Cousin-in-law, when you use words like forbid to me, smile!"
Serena sets Darrin straight.

[Episode #128, "HIPPIE, HIPPIE, HOORAY!"]

Cosmos Cotillion Cold Avocado Soup

2	medium Avocados
1	c. Milk (Cream, if you want it super rich and thick.)
½	c. Water, boiling
1	tsp. Chicken bouillon, granular
¼	tsp. Salt
	Pepper, to taste
¼	tsp. Garlic salt
1	Lemon, juice of
	Slices Lemon
	Paprika

Remove skin and seed from avocados. Dissolve bouillon in boiling water. Put avocado, milk, salt, pepper, garlic salt, lemon juice, and chicken bouillon in blender. Blend.

I prefer it thick, but to thin, just add more water or milk.

Float lemon slice on top of each bowl of soup and a sprinkle of paprika for color.

Serve by the pool with a small salad and croissant.

SERVES 2.

Serena: Well, it's almost 8:00! Shall we go over the song again?
Boyce: Gee, I don't think so, we've already done it twice. No use getting stale on it!

[Episode #192, "SERENA STOPS THE SHOW"]

Serena convinces Tommy Boyce, Bobby Hart, and their manager (Art Metrano) to sing her song at the Cosmos Cotillion.

[EPISODE #192, "Serena Stops the Show"]

I'm Gonna Blow You a Kiss in the Salad

What no cotillion should be without!

> **Buffalo mozzarella cheese (packed in water)**
> **Ripe tomatoes**
> **Fresh basil leaves, washed**
> **Extra virgin olive oil (First cold pressing is best.)**
> **Salt, to taste**
> **Pepper, to taste**

Slice cheese and tomatoes.

Overlap slices of cheese, tomato, and basil leaf. Repeat until sufficient.

Drizzle with olive oil. Sprinkle with salt and pepper if desired. Serve with following Galactic Garlic Toast.

Serena's Galactic Garlic Toast

French bread, sliced
Garlic cloves, sliced in half
Extra virgin olive oil (flavored, if desired)

From long loaf of French bread, cut as many slices as you like.
Slice clove, or cloves, of garlic in two.
Toast French bread slices (no butter).
Rub sliced side of fresh garlic over dry toast.
Drizzle with wonderful extra virgin olive oil.
That's it.

Loch Ness Mermaid Salad

2	Tbs. Lime juice
2	Tbs. Asian fish sauce* (I found this in the Specialty Department at the supermarket.)
1¾	tsp. Sugar
2	Jalapeño chilis, minced
1	Tbs. Lime, seeded and finely chopped (Include peel.)
1	6-oz. can Tuna, drained
1½	c. Jicama, peeled and julienned
½	c. Green onions, sliced
¼	c. Red pepper, minced
2	c. Iceberg lettuce, hand torn or shredded Cilantro, if you insist (this is the one herb I do *not* like).

Combine lime juice, fish sauce, sugar, and chilis in a bowl (cilantro, too, if you are using it).

Gently fold in all the other ingredients (except lettuce). Do not overmix.

Keep the tuna in bite-size chunks. Coat all with dressing.
Arrange lettuce on platter and top with the salad.
Zesty as Serena!
SERVES 2.

Serena: What's the matter? Haven't you ever seen a mermaid before?
Darrin: Yes. But only on a can of tuna!

[Episode #231, "SAMANTHA AND THE LOCH NESS MONSTER"]

Samantha: Compass point East and West and North, I beg the
Contessa Pirhana come forth!
Pirhana: (Popping in) You begged?

[Episode #245, "SERENA'S RICHCRAFT"]

More Cousin Trivia

In Episode #245, "Serena's Richcraft," the Contessa Pirhana (Ellen Weston) takes away Serena's powers. Who is Pirhana's aunt?
The High Priestess Hepzibah.

How many Witches/Warlocks sit on the Witches Council?
Eight. Samantha's spell in Episode #145, "It's So Nice to Have a Spouse Around the House," clearly says:

> "Witches Council, noble eight . . .
> Clearly hear me as I state,
> In haste I'll fly to do my task . . .
> But release the spell so I may ask!"

Name some of Serena's beauty marks!
That's right, she had a different one just about every time!
A heart, a peace sign, the universal symbol for women, a pair of lips, and an anchor!

COURTESY HERBIE J. PILATO COLLECTION

Having been temporarily stripped of her witchcraft by the Contessa Pirhana, Serena gets cozy with McMann and Tate client, Harrison Woolcott (Peter Lawford).

Contessa Pirhana's Cold Cherry Soup

2   c. Cherries, fresh and pitted
    (May use canned cherries in an emergency.)
½   c. Orange juice
½   c. Milk

Blend all in the blender. Chill and serve with little finger sandwiches. Real fingers.
SERVES 2 TO 3.

"Hi there, tall, dark and mortal!"

Serena greets Darrin, sort of one black sheep of the family to another!

[Episode #205, "DARRIN ON A PEDESTAL"]

Rock-a-Bye, Baby, to a Rock and Roll Beat,
Your pa is at the discotheque a-waggin' his seat,
Your ma's stringin' beads from her head to her feet!
So **Rock-a-Bye, Baby, to a Rock and Roll Beat!**

Another Serena original.

[Episode #128, "Hippie, Hippie Hooray"]

Rock-and-Roll Pineapple Salad

Scoop small curd cottage cheese on plate.
Cover with crushed pineapple (and a little juice).
Top with chopped walnuts.

Serena: Well, if you can do it, living the mortal life for us will be
   easy as falling off a log!
Samantha: And into the river and over the falls!

[Episode #165, "Samantha's Power Failure"]

Buck's Frozen Choco-Nuts-Nana's

Buck, the manager (Ron Masak), learned a valuable lesson the
day he hired Arthur and Serena to "roll and nut" the bananas:
Never hire anyone without references!

  1   **c. Coating chocolate (*no* other kind)**
  6   **Bananas**
  1   **c. Walnuts, chopped**
  6   **Wooden skewers**

Melt coating chocolate in top of double boiler over hot, not
boiling, water.
   Gently beat chocolate until cool to touch (80–85°F. on candy
thermometer).

Peel bananas. Insert wooden skewer in end. Dip into chocolate. Roll in chopped walnuts. Place on waxed paper in freezer until frozen. Wrap airtight in foil and return to freezer until ready to enjoy.

Ron Masak, who played Buck, the manager, recalls the day they shot the bananas on the conveyor belt routine.

"When we did the banana-chocolate-nut fight, Liz was pregnant at the time and fighting morning sickness. What a great trouper! She told me later that she couldn't eat chocolate for a long, long time."

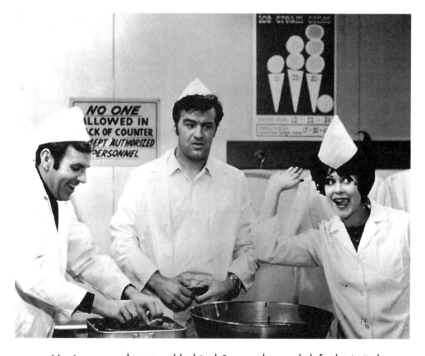

Having vowed to stand behind Samantha and defy the Witches Council, "Unky-poo" and Serena lose their powers and are forced to take real jobs. Bill Asher, who directed many episodes of "I Love Lucy," reenacted one of Lucy's famous bits for this hilarious scene from Episode #165, "SAMANTHA'S POWER FAILURE."

Serena: Moon Thatch Inn, where perfection reigns and, luckily, the sun never sets!

[Episode #145, "IT'S SO NICE TO HAVE A SPOUSE AROUND THE HOUSE"]

Moon Thatch Inn Coconut Cream Pie

A lovers' delight prepared specially by Madam Wageir (Fifi D'Orsay). Serena, having been taken to the Moon Thatch Inn by Darrin, *and* by mistake, stole this recipe from the very kitchens of Madam Wageir.

Crust

22	Gingersnap cookies
¼	c. Butter, melted
2	Tbs. Sugar

Crush Gingersnaps with rolling pin until fine crumbs. Mix in melted butter and sugar. Press against sides and bottom of an 8-inch pie plate. Chill.

Filling

1	pkg. Vanilla pudding mix
1½	c. Milk, cold
1	can (3½ oz.) Coconut, flaked
1	c. Cream dessert topping

Mix pudding mix and cold milk. Beat until mixture begins to thicken.

Stir in flaked coconut and cream dessert topping. Spoon into pie shell.

Chill again.

Decorate with more topping and light dusting of gingersnap crumbs.

Don't waste in a pie fight. Eatin's better.

"I'm sick of simmering like a watched pot, I wanna get out and boil!"

[Serena in Episode #111, "DOUBLE, DOUBLE, TOIL AND TROUBLE"]

Paramount Studio's Classic Reuben Sandwich

Serena once stormed Hollywood's gates, changed her name, and rented every billboard in town in order to blanket the movie industry! The closest she got to an acting job, however, was lunching on a Reuben Sandwich at the Paramount Studio commissary.

Rye bread
Sauerkraut, drained
Pastrami or corned beef thinly sliced (Chicken or turkey may be used, but the taste is more bland.)
Swiss cheese
Thousand Island Dressing

Spread dressing on one side of bread. Put 2 or 3 slices of meat across bread extending on either side.

Put 1 heaping spoonful of sauerkraut on meat.

Top with cheese. Bring sides of meat over to cover cheese.

Top with second piece of bread and grill until hot.

Samantha: Shhh! Serena may still be hanging around.
Darrin: I'm sure she is. Upside down from a rafter in the attic!

[Episode #189, "Tabatha's Very Own Samantha" Photo from Episode #155, "Serena Strikes Again"]

Dr. Bombay's Cuisine or

Around the World in 80 Decades with Dr. Bombay

A culinary journey of international cookery and helpful hints, many handwritten by Dr. Bombay himself.

> "From Tripoli to Timbuktu,
> I beg, I plead, I beseech of you
> A moment longer do not stay,
> Come to me, come to me, Dr. Bombay."

Samantha trying to contact TV's most effective physician!

[Episode #152, "Weep No More, My Willow"]

Dr. Bombay

Dr. Bombay is the galaxy's foremost leading witch doctor. To make an appointment simply call out "Paging Dr. Bombay! Paging Dr. Bombay! Emergency, come right away!" Nine times out of ten he'll show.

Hubert Bombay was taught medicine by Hippocrates. But by the mid 1800's, he briefly left his practice for the British Music Hall where he performed on the stage under many pseudonyms including George Leybourn, Albert Chevalier and Max Miller.

He returned to medicine at first to try and get even with Louis Pasteur for stealing his mold and marketing it to the mortal world as Penicillin! However, Bombay has made other great strides in the world of medicine, including cures for such ailments as Venetian Verbal Virus, Voracious Ravenositis, Metaphysical Molecular Disturbance, Gravititus Inflammitis and Bright Red Stripes Disease.

Some of his inventions have included the Atmospheric Oscillator which is a witch's way of witch-hunting (a device he's sure would have been a big mortal hit in 1692 Salem), and the Amber Corpuscular Evaluator, mandatory in the detection of Primary Vocabularyitis. Once diagnosed, Primary Vocabularyitis is easily treatable with painless sound wave injections, a fad among today's Pop Stars.

BERNARD FOX PRIVATE COLLECTION

Always possessing a penchant for the ladies, Bombay has personally trained over one hundred and seventeen thousand, nine hundred and forty-three voluptuous nurses during his long and illustrious career. He also enjoys riding in the Ostrich Derby, has planted his own flag on the top of Mount Everest, and even climbed the Matterhorn.

✳ Dr. Bombay Celebrates England's Boxing Day, Dec. 26th ✳

MENU

Witches' Wassail

Prime Rib and Dick York-shire Pudding

Green Beans Amandine

Weeping Willow Roly-Poly

✳

Witches' Wassail

1   qt. Apple cider
1   qt. Orange juice
¾   c. Lemon juice
1   pt. Cranberry juice
1   qt. Rum (optional)
1   tsp. Allspice
1   tsp. Whole cloves
3   Cinnamon sticks
¾   c. Sugar

Use 20–30 cup percolator. Put juices into the pot. Put spices and sugar in basket, and allow to perk slowly until flavors meld. Pour into punch bowl, and add rum.
YIELDS 16–20 CUPS.

Prime Rib

Almost foolproof, but a meat thermometer is essential.

1   **Prime Rib Roast (6 lbs. or larger)**

Preheat oven to 325°F. In shallow pan, stand roast on bone side, fat side up. Allow about 20 minutes per pound.

Trivia

The first role that Bernard Fox played in *Bewitched* was not Dr. Bombay, but modern-day witch hunter Osgood Rightmeyer in Episode #65, "Disappearing Samantha."

Roast is rare at 130°F., medium at 140°F., and well done at 160°F.

Remove roast when temperature reads 5°F. under desired temperature. Set aside. While roast is resting, it will continue to cook.

Osgood Rightmeyer: And now, my dear, I'm all yours.
Beverly (Carol Wayne): Oh, Mr. Rightmeyer!
Rightmeyer: Osgood.
Beverly: Ah's good, too!

[Episode #65, "Disappearing Samantha"]

Dick York-shire Pudding
(in Bombay's own inimitable words)

Goes well with Ye Olde Roast Beef of Ye Olde England

    1   scant cup Flour
        Pinch Salt
    2   Eggs
    1   cup Milk
        Drippings

Sift flour and salt into a basin. (Translation—"bowl.") Make a hole in the middle, and break eggs into the hole. Mix, adding milk, and beat into a smooth batter (about the consistency of half-and-half). The British prefer to put hot fat into a pan, but I get better and more consistent results by using Texas Muffin pans.

Put about a teaspoonful of the hot fat from the roast into each muffin hole, then pour in your York-shire mix to cover the bottom to about a quarter of an inch. Place your muffin pans in a 450°F. oven for 15 minutes, then reduce the heat to 350°F. for ten minutes or until the York-shire puffs up handsomely and is a golden brown. Serve with lashings of gravy.

Traditionally, the British serve the Yorkshire on its own, *be-*

fore the meat course. The idea being, if you stuff the guests with Yorkshire pudding, they won't be able to tackle so much meat! SERVES 6.

"I just remembered a pressing engagement with my tailor! A-Ha! A-Ha! A-Ha!"

A Bombastic Bombay Byword.

[Episode #200, "Make Love, Not Hate"]

Tailored Green Beans Amandine

1   lb. Fresh green beans
      Butter
1   bag Almonds, slivered
      Salt, to taste
      Pepper, to taste

Wash beans, snap off ends, and remove strings. Snap again into smaller lengths or slit lengthwise, julienne style.

Drop beans into large pot of boiling water. Boil gently 6 to 8 minutes or until just done. They should be *al dente*, slightly crunchy to the bite.

Drain and rinse in cold water to stop cooking.

To serve:

Melt butter in large skillet or pot. Add almonds. When butter and almonds are lightly browned, add the beans, salt, and pepper.

SERVES 3 TO 4.

* * *

> "Weeping willow, black with blight,
> I command with all my might
> Let your sap run free and bright.
> And, with every wayward breeze
> Which within your branches leap
> You will weep . . . and weep . . . and weep.

Water the patient daily, keep the neighborhood pets away . . . and pray!"

Bombay tries his hand at tree surgery.

[Episode #152, "WEEP NO MORE, MY WILLOW"]

Weeping Willow Roly-Poly

First you will need to know how to make a short-crust pastry. If you don't know, here's how:

Short Crust

4	c. Flour
1	tsp. Salt
½	c. Lard
½	c. Butter
	Cold water

Sift flour and salt; mix in butter and lard.
When well blended, add water to make a dry dough.

Jam Filling

Roll your short-crust pastry out and place in an oblong pan about 9 inches by 15 inches.

Spread with jam keeping it about half an inch from the edge so it doesn't squeeze out.

Roll the pastry up with the jam in it, and press edges together. Bake at 400°F. for approximately 30 to 40 minutes.

You can, of course, vary the ingredients, for instance, using a mince tart filling instead of jam, or pecan pie filling if you chop the pecans up fine.

You won't need all the short-crust pastry for this recipe, so cut the short-crust pastry recipe by half or make two Roly-Polys.

Malcolm Merryweather's Mincemeat*

3½ lb. Tart apples
8 c. Seedless raisins
2⅔ c. Currants
2 c. Orange peel, white membrane removed
1 tsp. Ground nutmeg
5 c. Sugar
1 c. Brandy or rum

Chop all the fruit finely or put through a mincer. Mix in the sugar, nutmeg, and brandy or rum.

Store in sterilized sealed jam jars. Yields about 20 8 oz jars.

✳ Dr. Bombay's "Make Love, Not Hate" Dinner ✳

MENU

Dr. Bombay's Devil's Punch Bowl

Hot with Passion Clam Dip

Colonel Crittendon's Stuffed Marrow

A Trifle with My Affections

---

*Once, having cured Mr. Merryweather of Cycle-Logical problems, he and Bombay have remained close friends.

Dr. Bombay's Devil's Punch Bowl

One glass of this and you'll make it Around the World in 80 Minutes.

4 qts. Dry apple cider (This cider is not sweet. If unavailable, Dr. Bombay substitutes dry champagne.)
1 fifth Orange Curaçao
1 fifth Cognac
1 squirt Lemon

"After imbibing this potion, the imbibee is smitten with the first person he sees. Of the opposite sex, of course!"

Dr. Bombay.

[Episode #200, "MAKE LOVE, NOT HATE"]

COURTESY BERNARD FOX PRIVATE COLLECTION

Mix 2 quarts dry apple cider (or champagne), ½ bottle Orange Curaçao and ½ bottle Cognac. Cut lemon in half and add a small squirt.

Sip slowly. *Very* slowly.

Reserve the other half of recipe for future date or refills—if you dare.

SERVES 40.

"I remember I was to squirt a lemon into the drink, but most of it shot out and hit Elizabeth in the eye and they yelled cut. The director said 'I bet you can't do that again,' and I did. Three times!"

[—B.F.]

Dr. Bombay: Where's the clam dip?
Samantha: (Pointing to kitchen sink) Over there.
Dr. Bombay: I may join him. I could do with a swim myself. A-HA! A-Ha! A-Ha . . . nothing.

Another Bombay original line.

[Episode #200, "MAKE LOVE, NOT HATE"]

Hot with Passion Clam Dip

½	lb. Crabmeat
8	oz. Cream cheese, softened
½	c. Sour cream
2	Tbs. Salad dressing (Different dressings give different flavors.)
1	Tbs. Lemon juice
1⅛	tsp. Worcestershire sauce
½	tsp. Dry mustard
	Garlic salt, to taste
	Milk
½	c. Cheddar cheese, grated
1	pinch Paprika

In a bowl, mix cream cheese, sour cream, salad dressing, lemon juice, Worcestershire sauce, mustard, and garlic salt until smooth. Add a little milk, just enough to make it creamy. Stir in 3 to 4 tablespoons of grated cheese.

Fold crabmeat into cream cheese mixture. Pour into greased casserole, (1 quart). Top with remaining cheese. Sprinkle paprika over.

Bake at 325°F. about 30 minutes, until bubbly and slightly browned.

Serve hot with crackers.

"Although Dr. Bombay was kind enough to give us the recipe for the clam dip, he was insistent that the love spell associated with it remain his secret and his alone. But he assured us that any one who didn't fall in love with this dip was himself a dip!"

[—K.R.]

Colonel Crittendon's Stuffed Marrow*

A favorite English dish of mine is "Stuffed Marrow." Marrow? you ask. Well, it looks like a green squash that has been allowed to get too big, but not so big that the skin has become tough. I got hold of some marrow seeds and grew my own, but we have since utilized overgrown squash, which has proved to be a very satisfactory substitute. Here's what you do.

Simmer the marrow (or squash) about seven minutes. Remove the marrow from the water and allow it to cool. Now take a slice off the large end and, with a long spoon, proceed to remove all the seeds and loose flesh. In England it would be stuffed with leftover minced lamb, beef, or whatever meat needed using up. However, we have found that any decent, meat loaf recipe works very well.

Stuff the meat loaf inside the marrow, tie on the piece you cut

*Having served together in World War II, the Colonel and the good doctor are close friends.

off, and, place in an oven pan with about a half inch of fat. Yes, fat! Sorry, but this is what makes it so delicious. Bake in a 350°F. oven, turning and basting every so often.

It's difficult to say how long it will take to cook because that depends on the size of the marrow or squash, but the meat loaf juices inside the marrow are flavoring the marrow flesh from the inside out, and basting with fat is doing the same thing from the outside in, for a magical caramelizing effect. You don't want the marrow to collapse, but it should be tender.

When I was playing Dr. Bombay on *Bewitched*, I gave Elizabeth Montgomery, who was a wonderful cook, one of my homegrown marrows, along with a recipe for the stuffing of same. A couple of days later, Bill Asher called me up to say that it was one of the best taste treats he had ever had!

[B.F.]

Endora: Samantha has lost her ZAP!
Bombay: Good! These mixed marriages . . . wouldn't have lasted anyway.
Endora: Not "SAP"! ZAP!

[Episode #113 "No Zip In My Zap"]

A Trifle with My Affections

	Cinnamon Gingerbread
2	cans Pear halves in juice
	Custard powder (Try instant custard or vanilla pudding, one or two large packages.)
Enough	Milk to mix with desired amount of pudding
	Whipping cream
	Flaked almonds for decoration
	Sherry (optional)

Line a large glass bowl with a deep layer of gingerbread. Drain the pears reserving the juice.

Cover the gingerbread with pears. If using sherry, mix to your taste with 1 or 2 cups of pear juice and pour onto pears.

Make enough custard to almost fill the rest of the bowl. Some will soak down through first two layers, so allow for that.

Place in refrigerator to set and cool.

When cool, cover with whipped cream and a sprinkling of almonds.

Sizes and measurements are all left open to personal preference. Since it's all so deliciously fattening, one might as well be generous with the things one likes!

"I remember in one scene I was brewing a cure for Samantha and the script called for a lock of hair. Elizabeth and I rehearsed it, and when it came time to shoot the scene I clipped the tiniest whisker of hair and all the crew gasped, saying "He clipped her hair!"

[—B.F.]

Samantha: If he can drink that, he's a Warlock, all right!

[Episode #65, "Disappearing Samantha"]

Osgood Rightmeyer's "Ordeal by Fire"

16   oz. Tomato juice
½   c. Vodka
2   Tbs. Lemon juice
1   tsp. Worcestershire sauce
    Dash Celery salt
    Dash Hot pepper sauce
    Dash Cayenne
    Sprinkle Red peppers
    Ice cubes
    Celery stalks

Stir together all ingredients, pour over ice, and garnish with celery stalk.

SERVE 3 TO 4.

Bombay: I haven't had a drink as good as that since Thursday!
Larry: "Thursday?"
Bombay: So am I! Let's have another drink!

[Episode #225, "Sam's Psychic Slip"]

Note: This old vaudeville gag was not original to the script. It was inserted into the episode by Bernard Fox.

[—M.W.]

Aunt Clara, Uncle Arthur, and Esmeralda

Aunt Clara

Samantha's Aunt Clara was never very good at the magical arts, a trait which became worse as she grew older. Many of her best feats of magic have been accidents, including the time she blacked out the entire Eastern Seaboard! Clara once inadvertently took Darrin, Samantha, Tabatha and Mrs. Kravitz on a jaunt to 1622 Plymouth for a Thanksgiving Dinner worth remembering

In 1950, Clara accidentally popped on to the Warner Bros. back lot. Alfred Hitchcock immediately cast her as Robert Walker's mother in his next picture, *Strangers on a Train*. Little did she know that she would one day be friends with one of her costars, Laura (soon to be Louise Tate) Elliot.

Clara is most proud of her extensive doorknob collection and insisted that it be mentioned in this book. "Polishing them is so soothing," she says.

✳ Aunt Clara's Accidental Thanksgiving to Remember ✳

MENU
Aunt Clara's Vaguely Definite Lemon Squares

Pilgrim Pie

Darrin's Puff-ed Butternut Squash

with

Apple and Orange Bread Stuffing

Clara's "Kale and Hardy" Concoction

Priscilla's Plymouth Pie

Indian Pudding with Nutmeg Hard Sauce

FROM THE COLLECTION OF KASEY ROGERS

TURKEY TIME

"Wings of falcon . . .
Turkey pull down,
Take us back . . .
to Plymouth Town!"
—Aunt Clara

[Episode #119, "Samantha's Thanksgiving to Remember"]

Gladys: I don't like this dream, it's too much work! Maybe it isn't a dream. But if it isn't a dream . . . what is it?

Mrs. Kravitz, convinced her Thanksgiving excursion is all in her head.

[Episode #119, "Samantha's Thanksgiving to Remember"]

Aunt Clara's Vaguely Definite Lemon Squares

1   c. Butter (or margarine)
2½   c. Flour
½   c. Powdered sugar

Sift flour and sugar together. Mix with butter. Lightly butter 9-by-13-inch cake pan. Press dough around bottom of pan to flatten. Puncture with a fork.

Preheat oven to 350°F. Bake for 20 minutes.

Meanwhile:

½   c. Real Lemon
1½   c. Sugar
4   large Eggs
4   Tbs. Flour
1   tsp. Baking powder

By hand, beat above ingredients together until sugar is dissolved. (Do not use electric mixer.)

Add:

1   tsp. Vanilla

Blend well. Pour over baked crust and bake for 20 minutes. Cool, sprinkle powdered sugar over top and cut into squares.

(Contributed by Joyce Steinman, Mark's mom's high-school pal.)

Pilgrim Pie

"Oh, what memories! The Pilgrims, Plymouth Rock . . . Miles Standish, Priscilla, John Alden . . . Boston Blackie!"

Aunt Clara remembers the first Thanksgiving . . . sort of!

[Episode #119, "SAMANTHA'S THANKSGIVING TO REMEMBER"]

Basic Pie Crust

See Esmeralda's Recipes, page 211 or prepared crusts are available at supermarkets.

1   9-inch pastry shell, unbaked

Vegetable Nut Filling

2   Tbs. Butter
1   c. Onions, chopped
½   c. Red bell pepper, chopped
4   c. Fresh spinach, coarsely chopped
¾   c. Pecans, chopped
1¼ c. Swiss cheese, grated
¼   c. Imitation bacon bits (optional)

1¼ c. Half-and-half
  3 **Eggs**
  ¾ **tsp. Salt**
  ⅛ **tsp. Black pepper, ground**

Prebake pastry shell at 425°F. for 10 minutes.
Melt butter in large skillet over medium heat.
Add onions and red peppers; sauté until clear.
Stir in spinach and sauté until wilted.
Sprinkle pecan pieces, cheese, and bacon bits (if desired) in bottom of pastry shell.
Spread spinach mixture over cheese layer.
Beat together half-and-half, eggs, salt, and pepper.
Pour into pie shell. Bake at 350°F. for 35 minutes, or until puffy and a knife inserted in center comes out clean. Do not overbake.
Slice and serve hot.

"All I had for breakfast was Puff-*ed* Rice."

Darrin attempts "Old English" at the table of John Alden.

[Episode #119, "Samantha's Thanksgiving to Remember"]

Aunt Clara: "I know I'm a little vague at times, but on the other hand, when I forget something I'm definite!"

[Episode #100, "Aunt Clara's Victoria Victory"]

Darrin's Puff-ed Butternut Squash with Apple and Orange Bread Stuffing

Allow ½ butternut squash per person.

Cut each squash in half. Scoop out and discard seeds and fibers.

Place in shallow baking dish, cut side up. Cover and bake at 350°F for 45 to 55 minutes or until easily pierced but not mushy.

When cool, scoop out pulp, leaving ½-inch-thick shells. Chop pulp.

Set pulp and shells aside.

Apple and Orange Bread Stuffing

2–3	c. Bread cubes
¼–½	c. Orange juice
¼	lb. Butter
2	c. Tart apples, diced
¼	c. Onions, diced
¼	c. Celery, diced
½	c. Orange, diced
2	tsp. Brown sugar (more for sweeter taste)
½	tsp. Cinnamon, ground
¼	tsp. Nutmeg, ground
2	tsp. Orange rind, grated
¼	c. Pine nuts (optional)

Pour orange juice over bread cubes. Toss and let stand 10 to 15 minutes.

Melt butter in skillet. Sauté apples, onions, celery.

Add orange pieces and brown sugar.

Cook slowly for 5 minutes over medium to low heat. If necessary, add a little more orange juice to prevent liquid from boiling away.

Remove from heat.

"That's two, count 'em, two bunches of fresh Kale!

Add bread cubes, cinnamon, nutmeg, orange rind, pine nuts, and chopped squash to mixture. Blend well.

YIELDS 4 TO 5 CUPS.

Now:

Line baking dish with foil.

Spoon stuffing mixture into squash halves and place in foil-lined baking dish.

Cover and bake until thoroughly heated, about 20–25 minutes.

Clara's "Kale and Hardy" Concoction

2   bunches Fresh kale
4   cloves Garlic, fresh
⅓   c. Olive oil or canola oil
4–6 Chilis, whole, dried
     Salt, to taste

Thoroughly wash the kale. Cut off stems and discard. Cut leaves into inch-wide strips.

Place kale in vegetable steamer. Steam for 10 minutes or until *al dente* (cooked, but not soggy).

While the kale is steaming, peel garlic and mince.

Into large frying pan, put olive oil, the garlic, and dried chilis (crushed with your fingers). Sauté until garlic turns light golden brown.

Remove from heat.

When kale is done, add to frying pan. Add a little more oil only if needed.

Mix well. Add salt and serve hot or cold.

Priscilla's Plymouth Pie

"Reminiscing about Plymouth has made me homesick for the girls I knew that settled there. I'd . . . uh . . . I'd like to visit them!"

Trouble begins to brew as Aunt Clara decides to celebrate Thanksgiving with some of her old girlfriends.

[Episode #119, "SAMANTHA'S THANKSGIVING TO REMEMBER"]

Pastry

2	c. All-purpose flour
½	tsp. Salt
⅔	c. Shortening
1	c. (4 oz.) Cheddar cheese (shredded)
6 to 8	Tbs. Ice water

Combine flour and salt. With pastry blender or 2 knives, cut in shortening until mixture looks like coarse crumbs. Mix in cheese. Sprinkle on ice water, tossing with fork until pastry is moist enough to hold together. Divide into 2 balls, one slightly larger. On lightly floured surface, roll larger piece into a 12-inch circle. Line 10-inch, deep-dish pie plate with pastry with a 1-inch overhang. Roll smaller piece into an 11-inch circle.

Preheat over to 450°F.

Filling

> 9 c. Apples, tart, peeled and sliced
> 1 Tbs. Lemon juice
> ¾ c. Pure maple syrup
> ¼ c. Brown sugar, firmly packed
> ¼ c. All-purpose flour
> ½ tsp. Cinnamon

Aunt Clara: "Now that you've gathered all the ingredients, the rest should be easy. Stand two feet away, concentrate and go for it! Now, repeat after me.

> 'Pinchly, finchly, freckle, toot!
> Pinch a freckle . . . one to boot!'

Did it work? Oh, well, maybe next time!"

Until then, mortal, proceed as follows.

In large bowl toss apples with lemon juice and syrup. Sprinkle on remaining ingredients and toss. Spoon filling into unbaked pie shell. Top with smaller pastry circle. Flute and cut vents.

In 450°F. oven, bake for 10 minutes. Lower heat to 375°F., and continue baking 50 to 60 minutes, until filling is tender.

Note: If pie browns too quickly, cover loosely with foil. This can be made ahead. Cool, wrap tightly, and freeze for up to 2 weeks. Thaw at room temperature 6 to 8 hours. Warm uncovered at 350°F. for 20 to 25 minutes, or enjoy piping hot straight from the oven.

Gladys: What do I do with this laundry bag?
Samantha: It isn't a laundry bag, it's a pudding bag! And we have to dip it in some boiling water.

[Episode #119, "Samantha's Thanksgiving to Remember"]

Indian Pudding with Nutmeg Hard Sauce

4   c. Milk
½   c. Yellow corn meal
½   c. Dark molasses
½   tsp. Salt
¼   c. Sugar
½   tsp. Ginger, ground
½   tsp. Cinnamon, ground
¼   c. Butter (or margarine)

Gradually, stir milk into corn meal. Cook over low heat, stirring constantly, until mixture comes to a boil. Add remaining ingredients, cooking over low heat, stirring constantly, for 15 minutes.

Preheat oven to 325°F. Bake in 1½-quart casserole for 1½ to 2 hours without stirring, until set. Serve hot with Nutmeg Sauce (recipe follows) and Hermits (recipe under Tabatha's Tea Party) or cream or ice cream.

SERVES 8 TO 10.

Nutmeg Hard Sauce (about 1¼ cups)

⅓   c. Butter
1   c. Confectioner's sugar, sifted
1   tsp. Vanilla extract
½   tsp. Nutmeg, ground

Cream the butter until light and fluffy. Gradually beat in sugar. Beat until very light and puffy. Beat in vanilla and nutmeg. Place a small spoonful of sauce on each serving of pudding.

✳   ✳   ✳

Clara's Trivia

What hobby did Aunt Clara and Marion Lorne have in common?

They both collected doorknobs. Marion's collection was used in numerous *Bewitched* episodes.

What were the names of Aunt Clara's beaus?

Hedley Partridge and Lord "Ocky" Ockum.

In Episode #83, "The Short Happy Circuit of Aunt Clara," the sound effect used for Aunt Clara coming down the chimney was the same as the one for Jeannie coming out of her bottle.

What was the name of Marion Lorne's first film in America?

You Hitchcock fans should've guessed it: *Strangers on a Train*. "Hitch" brought Marion over from England to play the part of Robert Walker's dithery mother.

> "In the park, all pink and new
> Polka dots of every hue
> Hear this wish, hear this chant
> Tabatha wants an el-e-phant."

Aunt Clara conjures up a pink, polka-dotted elephant for Tabatha.

[Episode #89, "A Gazebo Never Forgets"]

Aunt Clara's Pink and Polka-Dot Elephant

½ oz. gin
½ oz. Cherry brandy
¼ oz. Lemon juice
¼ oz. French vermouth
1 dash Orange bitters

Shake all with cracked ice. Strain into chilled cocktail glass.

＊　＊　＊

"Weebus, warbus, toodle, flick
Eat all this and you'll be sick."

Aunt Clara makes breakfast.

[Episode #118, "ALLERGIC TO MACEDONIAN DODO BIRDS"]

Pate de Foie Gras

Aunt Clara, having acquired all of Endora's powers, accidentally zaps up breakfast. The menu includes a live chef, Pate de Foie Gras, and champagne in Episode #118, "Allergic to Macedonian Dodo Birds."

1 Tbs. Butter
1 small clove Garlic, minced
2 Onions, finely chopped
½ lb. Goose livers (Chicken livers will do nicely, too.)
2 Tbs. Dry sherry
Pinch of Salt and pepper

Pinch   of Allspice, marjoram, and thyme (May substitute a
   dash of Worcestershire sauce.)
½   c. Butter

Combine butter, garlic, and onions. Sauté until onions are
soft. Add livers, and cook for 10 minutes. Put into a bowl and
mash with a fork. To the pan juices, add 2 or more tablespoons
dry sherry and the seasonings. Stir well, scraping down the skillet to get all the good brown bits. Add this to the liver mixture.
Stir until smooth. Cool.

Now, cream ½ cup of butter, stir in the liver mixture, and adjust seasoning. Add more sherry, if needed, to reach desired
consistently.

Pack into a small covered bowl or crock and refrigerate until
serving time.

Serve with little toast rounds or crackers.

YIELDS 1½ CUPS.

And, don't forget the champagne!

"And Long May You Wave:" "It was once told that Marion Lorne,
while in California to film an episode of *Bewitched,* called Elizabeth
to come over to her hotel room. She was quite excited. When Elizabeth got there, Marion insisted she could change the TV channels
magically! With a wave of her arm, she proceeded to prove it many
times!

Elizabeth didn't have the heart to tell Marion that when the metal
bracelets she was wearing clanged together they interrupted the re-
ception and caused the channel to change!

Frank: How did you know it [Coq au Vin] was my favorite dish?
Samantha: Oh, does Mrs. Stephens cook it for you?
Frank: Cook it? She can't even pronounce it.

[Episode #14, "SAMANTHA MEETS THE FOLKS"]

Coq au Vin

In Episode #14, "Samantha Meets the Folks," Aunt Clara turned Sam's Pot Roast into Coq au Vin, hoping it would impress Mrs. Stephens.

1	3-lb. Frying chicken, cut into pieces
¼	c. Butter
8	small Boiling onions, peeled
8	small Carrots, scraped
1	clove Garlic, minced
2	Tbs. Flour, all-purpose
2	c. Red wine, dry
1	Bay leaf
1	Tbs. Parsley, minced
¼	tsp. Savory, ground
¼	tsp. Thyme
1	can (4 oz.) Button mushrooms and liquid
1½	tsp. Salt (or less, to taste)
¼	tsp. Pepper

Have butcher quarter chicken or cut into smaller pieces. (If you cut chicken yourself, discard spinal cord and neck.)

Melt butter in a skillet, and brown chicken pieces over medium heat.

Remove chicken to a plate and set aside.

Add onions and carrots to skillet. Brown very lightly. Add garlic. Slowly stir in flour, then slowly stir in wine.

When wine is well blended, add bay leaf, parsley, savory, and thyme. Pour in liquid from can of mushrooms. Add salt and pepper.

Return chicken to pan and add mushrooms.

Cover and simmer slowly for 20 to 30 minutes, or until chicken and vegetables are tender.

Note: The better the wine, the better the dish.

SERVES 3 TO 4.

Clara: Now for dessert, Pineapple Upside Down Cake. It would be just my luck if it came up . . . right side up!

[Episode #14, "Samantha Meets the Folks"]

Aunt Clara's Pineapple (Hopefully) Upside Down Cake

1	box Yellow cake mix (your choice)
¼	c. Butter
1	c. Brown sugar
½	c. Chopped pecan nuts (optional)
1	8-oz. can Pineapple, sliced circles, drained
6	Maraschino cherries, no stems

Melt butter in a big old iron skillet or any cake pan. Spread brown sugar all over the bottom. If desired, sprinkle chopped nut meats evenly over bottom. Place rings of pineapple closely together covering bottom of pan. Place 1 maraschino cherry inside each pineapple ring, then . . .

Mix yellow cake batter according to directions on box. Pour cake mix over pineapple slices in baking pan and bake according to directions on box (or at 400°F. about 35 minutes). Top will be brown and crusty.

When *completely* cooled, turn out on a serving dish, fruit side up. Serve with whipped cream, if desired, but it really doesn't need it.

Variation: Try peaches and pecans instead of pineapple and cherries.

Ousted by an Ostrich! Jane Connell ("Queen Victoria," among others) had this to recount about Marion Lorne: "I remember she was doing a scene with an ostrich (a very dangerous bird), and they had cut. Everyone had gone about his business except for Marion, who was knee-deep in cables immobilized by the big bird! Bill [Asher], of course, was on his way to the phone when he noticed Marion's predicament. 'Would someone please go and rescue Marion?' he shouted to the crew."

✶ ✶ ✶

Aunt Clara's Pussy Willow Amandine Fudge

At the Annual Witches Cookout, in Episode #124, "Samantha's da Vinci Dilemma," Aunt Clara tried to make her favorite dish, "Sautéed Pussy Willow Amandine," but ended up with fudge and was unfortunately disqualified.

> 2 **c. Sugar**
> 1 **tsp. Cinnamon**
> ½ **tsp. Salt**
> 1 **c. Evaporated milk**
> 3 **Tbs. Butter**

Combine above ingredients and bring to a boil. Cook 5 minutes stirring constantly. Turn off heat.

Add first three ingredients. Reserve almonds.

> ⅓ **c. Miniature marshmallows**
> 1½ **c. Chocolate chips**
> 1 **tsp. Vanilla**
> **Whole almonds, garnish**

Stir until blended. Pour into buttered 8-inch pan and cool. Cut into squares and sprinkle with almonds.

YIELD 1½ POUNDS.

> "Colors lush and colors mellow . . .
> Kumquat orange and lemon yellow!
> Turpentine and brush of sable . . .
> Send to me, a painter able!"

Clara summons up Leonardo da Vinci from the great beyond!

[Episode #124, "SAMANTHA'S DA VINCI DILEMMA"]

Marion Lorne's last episode, #137, "SAMANTHA'S SECRET SAUCER," aired in April of 1968. Her last words of dialogue were, "But I'll be back." Marion left us May 9, 1968.

"Weebus, warbus, toodle fleck
. . . Uh . . . pinch a tag . . . No
. . . Pinch a walabus? . . .
. . . Oh, dear."

Aunt Clara accidentally conjures up two Jonathan Tates and tries to put them back together again.

[Episode #78, "ACCIDENTAL TWINS"]

Aunt Clara's Forgotten Cookies

2	Egg whites
⅓	c. Sugar, preferably superfine
Dash	Salt
1	c. Walnuts, chopped
1	c. Chocolate chips
1	tsp. Vanilla

Preheat oven to 350°F.

Beat egg whites until stiff. Add ⅓ cup sugar gradually while beating.

Add salt.

With a spoon, add the nuts and chocolate chips, then add the vanilla and mix well.

Put foil on cookie sheet. Drop mixture by the teaspoonfuls onto sheet.

When oven is hot, put cookie sheet into oven and *turn oven off.*

Now, just like Aunt Clara, *forget* about the cookies.

DO NOT PEEP. Leave in oven until morning.

Repeat **DO NOT PEEP.**

Best to prepare the night before you plan to serve them.

YIELDS 12.

UNCLE ARTHUR

Uncle Arthur

Baby brother of Endora, Clara, Hagatha and Enchantra, Arthur is the world's worst practical joker. Dubbed the "Clown Prince of the Cosmos" by Endora, Arthur is usually the only one amused by his antics, especially when he ruins dinner by appearing in it!

Arthur says his favorite practical joke was his "Yagga-Zuzi" spell. He had Darrin convinced that he could rid himself of Endora by using this spell (an impossible feat for a mortal). The plan, however, backfired on Arthur when Endora changed herself into a parrot to scare him! It worked. Arthur went on the wagon for about ten minutes! He has since used his "Yagga-Zuzzi" spell on several other mortals including Osgood Rightmeyer, an author of the occult. (Rightmeyer has not been seen since.)

Uncle Arthur has never been married, due to obvious reasons, but did come close once with a stuffy little witch named Aretha.

Bored with the jet set life of a Warlock, Arthur has most recently taken a job writing for David Letterman.

Arthur: "*Bon soir, mis a mis, Viva la France.* A scrumptious Napoleon
Now gets a chance . . . er, chaunce"

Uncle Arthur's head was not only in a stew, but when he tried to conjure up a French dessert, he got the real Napoleon!

[Episode #147, "Samantha's French Pastry"]

Samantha: When a Witch, or a Warlock, casts a spell involving an object, in this case a French pastry, the name of which may also be used to identify a human being, the kinetic vibrations run the risk of zonking across the atmospheric continuum, and the ectoplasmic manifestations which might not ordinarily occur—
Darrin: Sam! Sam!
Samantha: Yes, dear?
Darrin: I'm sorry I asked.

Samantha tries explaining the how's and why's of Arthur's Witchcraft blunder.

[Episode #147, "Samantha's French Pastry"]

"Endora, when I think of you as a blood relation, I long for a transfusion!"

[Arthur in Episode #165, "Samantha's Power Failure"]

"Yagga Zuzi, Yagga Zuzi, Yagga Zuzi Zim!
Zoom-a Zuzi, Zoom-a Zuzi, Zoom-a Zuzi Zim!
Zuzi- HI!
Zuzi-LO!
Zoom-a, Ooog-a, PITS!"

 "Forgive me for not rising, but I'm up to my neck in work!" says Uncle Arthur in his first episode, #41, "The Joker Is Card."

For Spell to work properly, don't forget the cow bell and duck call. And, by the way, it's "Zoo-zee"!

Uncle Arthur teaches Darrin a spell to ward off Endora's powers. Ha!!!

[Episode #41, "The Joker Is Card"]

Yagga Zuzi Fruit and Zuzi Cookies

3   lbs. Candied cherries, halves
2   lbs. Candied pineapple, chopped
5   qts. Pecans, halves and pieces
5   c. Flour

1   lb. Butter
2   c. Sugar
10 large Eggs, beaten
¾   c. Good whiskey (Wild Turkey, 86 proof)
1   tsp. Cloves
1   tsp. Cinnamon
1   tsp. Allspice
    Dash Ginger
    Dash Nutmeg

Sprinkle ½ cup flour over fruits and nuts. Set aside.

In large bowl, cream butter and sugar. Mix remainder of flour and all other ingredients into butter and sugar mixture. Add fruits and nuts.

Cover and let stand overnight.

Uncle Trivia:

In how many episodes of Bewitched does Paul Lynde appear?
Only ten! And he played Uncle Arthur in only nine!

In typical Bewitched fashion, Paul Lynde's first Bewitched appearance was not as Uncle Arthur. Who was he, and what was his occupation?
He played Harold Harold, Samantha's driving instructor in Episode #26, "Driving Is the Only Way to Fly."

Always the center of attention and often called a real square, what TV game show made Paul Lynde a household name?
The *Hollywood Squares*, in which he always sat in the center.

What is Endora's and Uncle Arthur's relationship?
Bad! Actually they are brother and sister as found out in Episode #80, "Endora Moves In for a Spell."

Drop by spoonfuls onto greased cookie sheet.

Cook at 275°F. for 30 minutes. If they start getting too brown, lower the temperature. They must have the full 30 minutes cooking time.

YIELDS APPROXIMATELY 100 COOKIES.

Uncle Arthur: "Oh, no, not an angel food cake. That's so cafeteria."

[Episode #147, "SAMANTHA'S FRENCH PASTRY"]

Arthur's Not-So-Cafeteria Devilish Angel Food Cake

¾   c. Cake flour (sift before measuring)
¼   c. Cocoa
1½   c. Sugar, very fine granulated
1¼   c. Egg whites
     Sprinkle Salt
1¼   tsp. Cream of tartar
1   tsp. Vanilla
¼   tsp. Almond extract

Sift flour, cocoa, and half the sugar (¾ cup) together two or three times for lightness.

Beat egg whites and salt until foamy. Sprinkle cream of tartar over egg whites and beat until stiff, not dry.

Sprinkle remaining sugar (¾ cup) over whites one tablespoonful at a time and fold in gently.

To egg white mixture, add vanilla and almond extract. Fold gently. Be sure sugar is dissolved.

Sift dry ingredients in gradually, folding as you go.

Turn batter into ungreased angel food cake pan (the ones that look a bit like a doughnut) and bake at 325°F. for 60 to 70 minutes.

Invert cake pan and cool for an hour.

Serve plain or with whipped cream, white or chocolate frosting, crushed strawberries, or whatever you dream up.

Oh, yes. If you leave out the ¼ cup cocoa and add ¼ cup flour, you will have a regular angel food cake.

Uncle Arthur: Looks like your angel food cake went to the devil.

Samantha: Thanks to you. You stepped on it!

Uncle Arthur: I did not. My feet weren't even in there! When you cast your spell, you probably faced west when you should have faced "yeast."

[Episode #147, "Samantha's French Pastry"]

Endora: Don't tempt me, little man, or I'll evaporate you!

Arthur: How'd you like to be turned into a half pint of sour cream?

[Episode #80, "Endora Moves in for a Spell"]

Arthur's Oh, So Tempting Sour Cream Pound Cake

6	Eggs, separated
½	lb. Butter (2 sticks)
3	c. Sugar
3	c. Flour, sifted
1	c. Sour cream
¼	tsp. Baking soda
	Pinch Salt
1	tsp. Vanilla extract
1	tsp. Lemon extract
1	tsp. Almond extract

Cream butter and sugar together; add egg yolks, one at a time.

Add flour and sour cream alternately, starting and ending with the flour.

Add baking soda, salt, and extracts.

Separately beat egg whites stiff and fold into the mixture.

Pour into tube pan or loaf pan that is greased, floured, and lined with waxed paper.

Bake at 300°F. for approximately 2 hours.

Uncle Arthur: Excuse me for not getting up, but my feet are killing me. (Two guns, attached to Arthur's shoes, fire at him!)

Louise: How nice. There's still some humor left in this world.

Samantha: Even if it's bad.

Yet another practical joke from the "I got a million of 'em" files of Uncle Arthur.

[Episode #150, "SAMANTHA LOSES HER VOICE"]

Arthur: One more word out of you and I'm leaving!

Darrin: Sorry.

Arthur: That's the word! (He *POPS* out.)

[Episode #147, "SAMANTHA'S FRENCH PASTRY"]

Uncle Arthur's Caribbean Banana Pop Out

After his short stint working with Serena in the mortal world (Episode #165, "Samantha's Power Failure"), Arthur found he liked bananas so much he created this little specialty for us.

¼   c. Butter, melted
4   medium Bananas
⅓   c. Brown sugar, packed
1½   Tbs. Lemon juice and grated peel
¼   tsp. Cinnamon
½   tsp. Allspice, ground
¼   c. Light rum (optional)

Place butter in baking dish; rotate dish to coat bottom.

Slice bananas in half, lengthwise. Place cut side down in baking dish.

Mix brown sugar, lemon juice and rind, cinnamon, and allspice.

Drizzle over bananas.

Bake uncovered in 350°F. oven for 15 minutes.

Heat rum until warm; ignite and pour over bananas.

SERVES 4.

"Screech Hoot Owls and Toot Ferry Boats . . . or is it 'Nanny Goats'?"

Uncle Arthur gets confused while trying to restore Samantha and Darrin's respective voices.

[Episode #150, "Samantha Loses Her Voice"]

Screech, Toot, Strawberry Hoot

1   c. Sugar
1   c. Water
1   3-oz. pkg. Strawberry Jell-O
    Fresh strawberries (In a pinch, use 1 10-oz. pkg. frozen strawberries.)
1   9-inch Graham Cracker Pie Crust
    Whipped cream or Cool Whip

Combine sugar, water, and Jell-O in boiler, and boil 3 minutes. Cool slightly.

Place deep layer of sliced strawberries on top of pie crust. Reserve a few whole strawberries for garnish.

Pour Jell-O mixture over strawberries. Cool in refrigerator until set.

Before serving, top with whipped cream or Cool Whip and accent with whole strawberries.

Graham Cracker Pie Crust

> 1½ c. Graham cracker crumbs
> ¼ to ½ c. Sugar
> ½ c. Butter, melted

Mix all ingredients well. Line 9-inch pie tin with mixture and press firmly with your fingers.

Bake at 375°F. for 8 minutes. Cool and fill.

Good crust for any fruit or cream pie.

ESMERALDA

Esmeralda

Shy and retiring, Esmeralda claims she has a raging Gloria Steinem deep inside! Esmeralda has never had a full grasp on anything, including witchcraft. When questioned about this she puts the blame on overly protective parents and a childhood destroyed by Mount Vesuvius.

Having her fiancé, Ramone Verona, the salad chef at the Warlock Club, leave her at the altar didn't help matters, either. Esmeralda ultimately fell back on former flame Ferdy and the two have enjoyed years of pleasant conversation together.

Still plagued by disaster-causing allergies, Esmeralda continues to work on coming out of her shell. This year alone, through the miracles of modern "plastic sorcery," she has turned herself into Barbara Walters and appears on TV regularly.

Darrin: We are talking about an omelet made with chicken eggs?
Esmeralda: We are? All right, if that's the way you want it!

[Episode #208, "Samantha's Old Salem Trip"]

Esmeralda's Spanish Omelet

Important that Spanish Omelet be prepared while wearing a Flamenco dress and mantilla!

Allow 1 or 2 eggs per omelet. Best to cook one at a time in a Teflon coated pan.

Pterydactyl Eggs (If unavailable, use boring chicken ones.)
Butter
Onions, chopped
Green pepper, chopped
Garlic, minced
Salt, pepper
Dash of Tabasco (optional)
Cheddar cheese, shredded

Melt butter in pan. Add chopped onions, green pepper, and garlic. Sauté until translucent.

Break eggs into bowl, sprinkle with salt, pepper, and dash of Tabasco (optional); then stir briskly.

Pour egg mixture into pan and shake back and forth. Lift edges that have cooked so liquid eggs will run over.

Shake back and forth again. Lift edges again if necessary.

Sprinkle omelet with shredded Cheddar cheese and allow to melt a little.

Do not overcook. Fifteen seconds should be enough time.

Slide omelet onto plate, folding over as you go.

Spoon Spanish-on-the-Side Salsa over omelet.

Esmeralda: How do you feel about a plain omelet, with Spanish on the side?

[Episode #208, "Samantha's Old Salem Trip"]

Spanish-on-the-Side Salsa

Don't forget the castanets!

2–4	Tomatoes, seeded, drained, and chopped
½	c. Green onions, thinly sliced
4	oz. Canned green chilis, seeded, chopped
1	tsp. Lemon peel, grated (optional)
½	tsp. Salt
¼	tsp. Garlic salt
⅛	tsp. Pepper
½	tsp. Oregano, dried, crushed
2–3	Tbs. Lemon juice
2	Tbs. Olive oil

Mix all ingredients in large bowl. Cover and refrigerate several hours to meld flavors.

To serve: Warm, then spoon over omelet.

Note: Cold salsa is great as a dip, with tortilla chips.

Esmeralda's Tower Special

"One Tower, and make it lean!" conjures Esmeralda, causing Pisa's most famous building to take on its undeniably famous characteristic.

8	slices Of some wonderful Italian bread
8–16	slices Roast beef
8–16	slices Turkey breast
8	slices Swiss cheese
8–16	spears Asparagus (or broccoli)
	Rings Onion, raw
	Pisa Rarebit (Recipe follows.)
	Butter

Sesame seed or cayenne and parsley sprigs (for garnish)

Steam asparagus until just tender.

Pisa Rarebit (Later Stolen by the Welsh!)

(May be divided for smaller quantities.)

1 **lb. Sharp Cheddar cheese, diced**
2 **Tbs. Butter**
1 **tsp. Dry mustard**
   Cayenne pepper, to taste
2 **Eggs, slightly beaten**
   Salt, to taste
1 **c. Beer**

In top of double boiler, or chafing dish, combine the cheese, butter, mustard, and cayenne pepper.

Cook gently over low heat, stirring constantly, so as not to "seize" the cheese. When melted, beat a little of the hot cheese mixture into the eggs. Return mixture to the pan. Sprinkle with salt. Add the beer and cook another couple of minutes, until very hot but not boiling.

To assemble:

Butter and toast the bread. Place toasted sides upon individual plates.

Pile roast beef, Swiss cheese, turkey, onion rings, and asparagus on each slice. Repeat until Tower is leaning. Just be sure your eyes are not larger than your tummy.

Spoon generous portion of Pisa Rarebit over all and sprinkle with sesame seeds, cayenne, and sprig of parsley.

Hardy!

Count Bracini: You will do me the honor of having dinner with me?
Esmeralda: Now? Before Lunch?!

Count Bracini invites *amour*-struck Esmeralda to an Italian evening.

[Episode #232, "Samantha's Not-So-Leaning Tower of Pisa"]

Double, Double Bubble and Squeak

Esmeralda can't remember whether she borrowed this recipe from Aunt Clara or Dr. Bombay, but it's very British.

1	**Cooked potato**
½	**c. Cooked greens (or sprouts or cabbage, etc.)**
1	**Tbs. Fat for frying**
1	**small Finely sliced onion**
	Salt and pepper

Fry all the ingredients very slowly and gently in fat. Salt and pepper to taste. Serve hot.

✳   ✳   ✳

"I was almost kissed by a king, but I sneezed right in the middle of it! It took them two days to find him!"

Tabatha asks Esmeralda if a prince had ever kissed her.

[Episode #172, "Samantha's Yoo-Hoo Maid"]

POTATO PARLAY FIT FOR A PRINCE

A good maid, Witch or not, knows the value of the potato, and Esmeralda could work her magic by stretching the not-so-lowly spud further than anyone.

Double Stuffed Potatoes

6 Baked Idaho potatoes
4 Tbs. Butter
½ c. Milk (more or less to make smooth)
   Salt, to taste
   Pepper, to taste
1 pt. Sour cream (optional)
1½ c. Green onions, chopped,
1½ c. Sliced, dried beef chopped (It comes in jars.)
1½ c. Cheddar cheese, grated
   Sprinkle Parmesan or Romano grated cheese
   Sprinkle Paprika (optional)

Lengthwise, cut off top ⅓ of the baked potatoes.

Scoop out large sections leaving ¼ to ½ inch of potato in shell. Scoop out small sections leaving ¼ inch of potato in shell. Set shells aside.

Mash potatoes with butter, milk, salt, and pepper.

Add chopped green onions, chipped beef, grated Cheddar, (and Sour cream, if you want to be really naughty). Mix well.

Refill large shells. Top with liberal sprinkle of Parmesan or Romano cheese and dusting of paprika for color.

Rebake at 350°F. for 30 minutes. Turn oven to 375°F. and continue baking for 5 minutes or until tips of potatoes are browned.

✳   ✳   ✳

Attracted to you! When Alice Ghostley was asked why she didn't drive, she replied, "I got my driver's license once, and suddenly solid objects became magnets! I ran into every fence and tree in sight. Unlike the walls in *Bewitched*, I couldn't fade through them!"

✳   ✳   ✳

"I wonder if that's what they mean by life, liberty, and the happiness of pursuit," sighs Esmeralda as intended beau, Norton, (Cliff Norton) chases after Samantha instead.

[Episode #200, "Make Love, Not Hate"]

In Pursuit of the Perfect Potato

Remember top ⅓ potatoes you reserved?

6	small tops Baked potato shells
6	Tbs. Cheddar cheese, fresh grated
6	Tbs. Romano cheese, fresh grated
6	Tbs. Green onions, chopped
3 or 4	slices Bacon, fried crisp and crumbled
	Salsa, hot or mild
	Sour cream (optional)

Cut each ⅓ top shell into four smaller pieces.

Mix grated Cheddar and Romano cheeses, chopped green onions, and bacon bits.

(For crisper shells, bake empty shells in preheated 350°F. oven for 10 minutes first.)

Then fill shells with cheese mixture and broil about 10 minutes until cheese is melted.

Serve as appetizer with salsa and sour cream on the side.

"Top Tiger Cologne, the reason why Cleopatra let Julius "Seize her"!

Darrin's slogan for client Evelyn Charday.

[Episode #173, "Samantha's Caesar Salad"]

Top Tiger Tater Tots!

A favorite of Top Tiger Cologne CEO, Evelyn Charday (Joyce Easton).

Leftover mashed potatoes may be formed into small balls and sautéed in butter for breakfast (with bacon and eggs). Even go with dinner.

Mother Goose: And they said "Hey Diddle, Diddle" wouldn't last!
Samantha: Well, what do "they" know?!

Mother Goose's Shoofly Pie

Basic Pastry Crust

> 1   c. + 2 Tbs. Pastry flour, white or whole wheat
> ⅓   tsp. Salt
> ⅓   c. Butter, very cold, salted or unsalted and cut into bits (Regular shortening may be used.)
> 5–6   Tbs. Ice Water

Combine flour and salt in mixing bowl. Cut in butter with pastry blender or two knives until it looks like little peas. Do not overmix. Leave a little chunky for a flaky crust.

Then, add one tablespoon of ice water at a time and toss lightly with a fork until pastry dough will hold together when pressed gently into a ball.

Cover and chill dough for a half hour or longer.

On a well-floured board, roll dough out two inches larger than your pie pan. Line pan with crust, trim and crimp edges.

Fill pie shell and bake as directed in recipe,

Or,

for partially baked pie shell, bake only 10 minutes at 425°F., then proceed with direction of filling recipe.

Or,

for prebaked pie shell, preheat oven to 425°F., prick bottom of pie shell generously with a fork and bake for 16 to 18 minutes.

Note: During baking, open door a couple of times to see if crust is bubbling in spots. Puncture or push down gently to produce flat crust.

Crumbs

1½   c. All-purpose flour
2   Tbs. Butter
½   c. Brown sugar, firmly packed
     Salt, to taste
1   tsp. Cinnamon

Mix all ingredients together in a large bowl until it looks like large crumbs. Set aside.

Filling

½   c. Molasses
½   c. Boiling water
1   tsp. Baking soda
¼   tsp. Ginger, ground

In a bowl, combine molasses and water, then stir in baking soda and ginger.

To assemble:

Heat oven to 350°F.

Mix ¾ of the crumbs with filling and pour into unbaked pie shell.

Sprinkle the rest of the crumbs on top.

Bake about 30 minutes. Should be golden brown.

Trivia

Can you name some of Esmeralda's beaus:
Ramone Verona (Salad Chef at the Warlock Club), Ferdy (Tom Bosley), Bonano Pisano (Robert Casper), Norton (Cliff Norton).

How many episodes did Alice Ghostley make?
Sixteen. But only 15 were as Esmeralda.

Always seeming to be cast as a maid, can you name Alice's first Bewitching maid character?
Naomi, the mortal maid in Episode #53, "Maid to Order"

"A mother-in-law and a Mother Goose in the same house are too much 'mother'!"

Samantha to a fading Esmeralda.

[Episode #182, "Samantha's Double Mother Trouble"]

Hey! Diddle, Diddle! and Apple Pan Dowdy

Preheat oven to 350°F.

3   c. Granny Smith (or other tart) apples, peeled

Slice into buttered baking dish.

½   c. Molasses
¼   tsp. Nutmeg
½   tsp. Cinnamon
¼   tsp. Salt

Mix these ingredients together. Then sprinkle over apples and bake apples until soft.

1   box Cake mix (your choice of flavors)
Whipped cream

Prepare according to directions on box. Pour batter over apples and continue baking until cake is done.

Turn out apples on top of cake and top hot apples with whipped cream.

> "Shoofly Pie and
> Apple Pan Dowdy!
> Make your eyes light up
> Your tummy say 'howdy.' "

Esmeralda used to try this spell constantly until Samantha told her it was just the lyrics from an old song inspired by Dutch/Southern recipes.

> "As the trumpets sound
> With a shimmering beat,
> She who drinks this,
> Will crave to eat!"

Esmeralda hexes Tabatha's milk in order to get her to eat. The only trouble is, Sam drinks it by mistake, causing a severe bout with Voracious Ravenousitis.

[Episode #186, "SAMANTHA'S LOST WEEKEND"]

Esmeralda's Specialty of the House Coffee with Milk

An intimate concoction for 30.

To 3 cups boiling water, add the following ingredients in large pot and cool overnight:

> ¼   **c. Sugar**
> 4½ **Tbs. Instant coffee**
> 6   **Tbs. Chocolate syrup**
> ¼   **tsp. Salt**

When ready to serve, add to the cooled mixture:

> 1   **tsp. Vanilla**
> 1   **qt. Milk**

In punch bowl, pour above mixture over:

> ½   **gal. Vanilla ice cream, softened**

Over ice cream, pour:

> 1   **qt. Ginger Ale**

Mix with ladle and serve.

There's No Place like Home: Louise Tate, Dr. Bombay, and Gladys Kravitz revisit the old neighborhood February 2, 1995.

Bewitched

CAST LIST

Samantha/Serena	Elizabeth Montgomery
Darrin Stephens	Dick York (1964–1969)
	Dick Sargent (1969–1972)
Endora	Agnes Moorehead
Maurice	Maurice Evans
Tabatha	Erin Murphy
	Diane Murphy
Adam	David Lawrence
	Greg Lawrence
Larry Tate	David White
Louise Tate	Irene Vernon (1964–1966)
	Kasey Rogers (1966–1972)
Gladys Kravitz	Alice Pearce (1964–1966)
	Sandra Gould (1966–1972)
Abner Kravitz	George Tobias
Aunt Clara	Marion Lorne (1964–1968)
Uncle Arthur	Paul Lynde (1965–1972)
Phyllis Stephens	Mabel Albertson
Frank Stephens	Robert F. Simon
	Roy Roberts
Esmeralda	Alice Ghostley (1969–1972)
Dr. Bombay	Bernard Fox (1967–1972)

Bewitched

EPISODE GUIDE

by Steven Colbert

Our gratitude and appreciation, not only for the Episode Guide, but all the wonderful work and many contributions Steven Colbert has made to *The* Bewitched *Cookbook—Magic in the Kitchen.*

[—K.R. & M.W.]

The First Season, 1964–65

<small>EPISODES:</small>

#1 **"I, Darrin, Take This Witch, Samantha"** 9/17/64
Following marriage to Darrin, Samantha faces off with his former girlfriend, Sheila, and makes a shambles of her dinner party and dignity.

#2 **"Be It Ever So Mortgaged"** 9/24/64
Samantha and Endora have big plans for the new house much to the surprise of snoopy neighbor, Gladys Kravitz.

#3 **"It Shouldn't Happen to a Dog"** 10/1/64
A client's bark is far worse than his bite after Samantha diffuses his advances by turning him into a puppy dog.

#4 **"Mother Meets What's-His-Name"** 10/8/64
Darrin nervously prepares to meet his bewitching mother-in-law for the first time. Little does he suspect what's in store.

#5 **"Help, Help, Don't Save Me"** 10/15/64
Darrin thinks Samantha's slogans for Caldwell Soup are the result of witchcraft.

#6 **"Little Pitchers Have Big Fears"** 10/22/64
Samantha helps a Little Leaguer make the team against the wishes of his overprotective mother.

#7 **"The Witches Are Out"** 10/29/64
Samantha and her witchly clan try to improve their image on Halloween after Darrin's client depicts them as ugly old hags.

#8 **"The Girl Reporter"** 11/5/64
Samantha is jealous of the college girl assigned to interview Darrin for her school paper.

#9 **"Witch or Wife"** 11/12/64
Samantha's luncheon in Paris with Endora gets her into big trouble with Darrin and the Tates.

#10 **"Just One Happy Family"** 11/19/64
An angry Maurice takes action when he learns that his daughter has married a mortal.

#11 **"It Takes One to Know One"** 11/26/64
Endora tests Darrin's fidelity by providing a "Miss Jasmine" needed for a perfume account.

#12 **". . . And Something Makes Three"** 12/3/64
Larry gets the surprise of his life when the baby announcement he thinks will be Samantha's is really Louise's.

#13 **"Love Is Blind"**   **12/10/64**
Darrin is reluctant to fix his friend, Kermit, up with Samantha's friend, Gertrude, fearing that she may be a witch.

#14 **"Samantha Meets the Folks"**   **12/17/64**
Samantha hopes to make a favorable impression during her first meeting with Darrin's parents.

#15 **"A Vision of Sugar Plums"**   **12/24/64**
The Stephens invite a lonely orphan home for the holidays to teach him the true meaning of Christmas.

#16 **"It's Magic"**   **1/7/65**
Samantha assists a washed-out magician at the hospital benefit.

#17 **"A Is for Aardvark"**   **1/14/65**
A bed-ridden Darrin gets a taste of power after Samantha convinces him to sample the magical life.

#18 **"The Cat's Meow"**   **1/21/65**
The head of a cosmetics firm takes an interest in Darrin for more than just his ad campaign.

#19 **"A Nice Little Dinner Party"**   **1/28/65**
Darrin's mother, Phyllis, thinks her marriage is in trouble when her husband, Frank, takes an interest in Endora.

#20 **"Your Witch Is Showing"**   **2/4/65**
Darrin has a run of bad luck at work after he forbids Samantha to go to Egypt with Endora for a wedding.

#21 **"Ling Ling"**   **2/11/65**
Samantha turns a Siamese cat into a glamorous model for Darrin's "Jewel of the East" campaign.

#22 **"Eye of the Beholder"**   **2/25/65**
Darrin's discovery of Samantha's real age has him worried about their future.

#23   "Red Light, Green Light"   3/4/65
Samantha resorts to magical tactics to get a traffic light installed at a busy intersection.

#24   "Which Witch Is Which?"   3/11/65
While posing as Samantha's look-alike for a dress fitting, Endora wins the affections of an author-friend of Darrin.

#25   "Pleasure O'Reilly"   3/18/65
Darrin's friendship with the beauty queen who moved in next door, infuriates her very jealous boyfriend.

#26   "Driving Is the Only Way to Fly"   3/25/65
Samantha tries to learn to drive without the use of witchcraft.

#27   "There's No Witch Like an Old Witch"   4/1/65
Aunt Clara's baby-sitting skills prove very entertaining for the children, but leave a lot to be desired by their parents.

#28   "Open the Door Witchcraft"   4/8/65
An electric garage door opener causes trouble for Darrin and Samantha.

#29   "Abner Kadabra"   4/15/65
Neighbor Gladys Kravitz is convinced she has magical powers after she catches Samantha in a weak moment.

#30   "George, the Warlock"   4/22/65
Endora summons an ex-beau of Samantha's, hoping he can whisk her away from Darrin.

#31   "That Was My Wife"   4/29/65
Larry suspects Darrin is having an affair after he is spotted in a hotel lobby with a dark-haired woman. The woman is actually Samantha in a black wig.

#32   "Illegal Separation"   5/6/65
Abner takes up residence at the Stephens' house after he and Gladys have a fight.

#33   "A Change of Face"   5/13/65
Darrin's ego is in need of a boost after Samantha and Endora temporarily reconstruct his face.

#34   "Remember the Main"   5/20/65
Samantha helps a local politician boot his crooked opponent out of office.

#35   "Eat at Mario's"   5/27/65
Samantha and Endora promote a local Italian restaurant while McMann and Tate's newest client is its competitor—a large pizza chain.

#36   "Cousin Edgar"   6/3/65
Samantha's overprotective cousin has it in for Darrin until he realizes how happy the pair are.

The Second Season, 1965–66

#37   "Alias Darrin Stephens"   9/16/65
Aunt Clara accidentally turns Darrin into a chimpanzee. When he is changed back, Samantha announces that they are going to have a baby.

#38   "A Very Special Delivery"   9/23/65
Samantha may be pregnant, but it's Darrin who has morning sickness, thanks to Endora's spell.

#39   "We're In for a Bad Spell"   9/30/65
Aunt Clara helps Samantha undo a curse that was placed on an ancestor of Darrin's friend.

#40   "My Grandson, The Warlock"   10/7/65
Maurice thinks that the baby Samantha is temporarily caring for is his grandson, when in reality it's Larry and Louise Tate's.

#41   "The Joker Is Card"   10/14/65
    The joke is on Darrin when Samantha's Uncle Arthur teaches him some "special" magic to use against Endora.

**#42   "Take Two Asprin and Half a Pint of Porpoise Milk"
10/21/65**
    Aunt Clara tries to cure Samantha when her face breaks out with square green spots.

#43   "Trick-or-Treat"   10/28/65
    Halloween takes a turn for the hairy when Endora changes Darrin into a werewolf!

#44   "The Very Informal Dress"   11/4/65
    At a cocktail party things get embarrassing for Darrin and Samantha when clothes conjured up for them by Aunt Clara begin to vanish.

#45   "And Then I Wrote"   11/11/65
    Samantha's characters literally come to life when she is assigned to write a play about the Civil War.

#46   "Junior Executive"   11/18/65
    Darrin gets a second childhood after Endora turns him into an eight-year-old boy.

#47   "Aunt Clara's Old Flame"   11/25/65
    Aunt Clara is insecure about a reunion with former beau Hedley Partridge.

#48   "A Strange Little Visitor"   12/2/65
    A ten-year-old-Warlock spends the weekend with Darrin and Samantha.

#49   "My Boss the Teddy Bear"   12/9/65
    Darrin accuses Endora of changing Larry Tate into a stuffed teddy bear.

#50   **"Speak the Truth"**   12/16/65
   The truth is more than anyone can bear when Endora's magic statue causes anyone who comes near it to speak his or her mind.

#51   **"A Vision of Sugar Plums"**   12/23/65
   A recut version of Episode #15—new opening.

#52   **"The Magic Cabin"**   12/30/65
   Samantha magically restores a rustic old cabin—of Larry's—for a newlywed couple searching for a home.

#53   **"Maid to Order"**   1/6/66
   Samantha hires a maid whose cooking and cleaning talents need a witchly boost.

#54   **"And Then There Were Three"**   1/13/66
   Darrin mistakes Serena for a grown-up version of his newborn daughter, Tabatha.

#55   **"My Baby the Tycoon"**   1/20/66
   A suspicious Darrin accuses baby Tabatha of being able to rattle the stock market.

#56   **"Samantha Meets the Folks"**   1/27/66
   A recut version of Episode #14 with a new opening.

#57   **"Fastest Gun on Madison Avenue"**   2/3/66
   Darrin makes the headlines when he knocks out a heavyweight boxer . . . with some help from Samantha.

#58   **"The Dancing Bear"**   2/10/66
   It's a battle of the in-laws when Endora and Darrin's parents come to visit the new baby.

#59   **"Double Take"**   2/17/66
   Darrin becomes his own boss after Endora grants him three wishes without his knowledge.

#60 "Samantha, the Dressmaker"   2/24/66
Samantha "borrows" some ideas for a homemade dress from a French designer who happens to be Darrin's client.

#61 "The Horses's Mouth"   3/3/66
Samantha changes a runaway race horse into a woman to persuade her to start winning races.

#62 "Baby's First Paragraph"   3/10/66
Tabatha has the last word after Endora gives the infant the ability to talk.

#63 "The Leprechaun"   3/17/66
A leprechaun seeks Samantha's help for the recovery of his lost pot of gold.

#64 "Double Split"   3/24/66
Samantha's treatment of a client's rude daughter causes Darrin and Larry to have a fight.

#65 "Disappearing Samantha"   4/7/66
An anti-witch client of Darrin's claims that they are neurotic bores.

#66 "Follow That Witch," Part 1   4/14/66
An overly suspicious client is having Darrin and Samantha investigated.

#67 "Follow That Witch," Part 2   4/21/66
A private detective uses blackmail tactics to get magical favors from Samantha.

#68 "A Bum Raps"   4/28/66
A street bum poses as Darrin's Uncle Albert to win Samantha's hospitality.

#69 "Divided, He Falls"   5/5/66
Endora divides Darrin so that he can simultaneously take a vacation and work on an important ad campaign.

#70 **"Man's Best Friend"**   **5/12/66**
A former ex-suitor of Samantha returns as a dog in order to be near her when Darrin's around.

#71 **"The Catnapper"**   **5/19/66**
Endora changes Darrin's attractive client into a cat.

#72 **"What Every Young Man Should Know"**   **5/26/66**
The Stephens go back in time to find out if Darrin would have knowingly married a witch.

#73 **"The Girl with the Golden Nose"**   **6/2/66**
Darrin thinks Samantha helped him win the account that enabled him to buy her a mink coat.

#74 **"Prodigy"**   **6/9/66**
Samantha helps a nervous violin prodigy return to the concert stage after an embarrassing childhood incident damaged his career.

The Third Season, 1966–67

#75 **"Nobody's Perfect"**   **9/15/66**
Samantha discovers that Tabatha is a full-fledged Witch and tries to keep it from Darrin and Endora.

#76 **"The Moment of Truth"**   **9/22/66**
Darrin learns that Tabatha is a witch during a dinner party with the Tates.
Note: Kasey Rogers makes her debut as "Louise" in this episode.

#77 **"Witches and Warlocks Are My Favorite Things"**
9/29/66
A coven of witches convenes at the Stephens' house as Tabatha's powers are put to the test.

#78 **"Accidental Twins"**   **10/6/66**
Bumbling Aunt Clara conjures up a double of the Tates' little Jonathan and has trouble reversing the spell.

#79 "A Most Unusual Wood Nymph"   10/13/66
Samantha travels back in time to the days of Darrin the Bold to undo a curse placed on Darrin and his ancestors.

#80 "Endora Moves In for a Spell"   10/20/66
Endora takes up residence on the block to keep tabs on Uncle Arthur and his magical pranks.

#81 "Twitch or Treat"   10/27/66
The Stephens' home is the setting for Endora's Halloween party, whose guests are among the witch community's most elite.

#82 "Dangerous Diaper Dan"   11/3/66
A diaper man moonlights as a spy for a McMann and Tate rival by planting a bug in a rattle he gives to Tabatha.

#83 "The Short Happy Circuit of Aunt Clara"   11/10/66
Everyone is left in the dark after Aunt Clara accidentally causes a power failure across the entire Eastern Seaboard.

#84 "I'd Rather Twitch Than Fight"   11/17/66
Samantha and Darrin separately seek advice from psychiatrists, with both doctors having different ideas of achieving marital harmony.

#85 "Oedipus Hex"   11/24/66
The work ethic goes out the window when a hexed bowl of popcorn conjured up by Endora causes Darrin and his friends to become lazy couch potatoes.

#86 "Sam's Spooky Chair"   12/1/66
A magical chair acquired by Samantha actually turns out to be Clyde Farnsworth, a warlock from her past who's still in love with her.

#87 "My Friend Ben"   12/8/66
Benjamin Franklin pays a visit to the twentieth century when Aunt Clara summons an electrician to fix a lamp. (Part 1 of 2.)

#88 **"Samantha for the Defense"**   12/15/66
Ben Franklin faces charges of grand theft for accidentally driving off in a fire engine that bears his name. (Part
2 of 2.)

#89 **"A Gazebo Never Forgets"**   12/22/66
A pink and purple elephant roams the house, thanks
to Aunt Clara, as Samantha tries to impress a bank president to get a loan.

#90 **"Soap Box Derby"**   12/29/66
Samantha helps a twelve-year-old boy enter and win a
soapbox derby without informing the boy's father, a me-
chanic.

#91 **"Sam in the Moon"**   1/5/67
Samantha has a hard time convincing Darrin that she
did not go to the moon, but instead went shopping in
Tokyo with Endora.

#92 **"Ho, Ho, the Clown"**   1/12/67
Tabatha becomes the object of a TV clown's affections,
thanks to a spell by Endora.

#93 **"Super Car"**   1/19/67
Darrin's got the hottest wheels on the block after Endora zaps up a prototype car from a magazine for him.

#94 **"The Corn Is as High as a Guernsey's Eye"**   1/26/67
Feeling like a failure as a witch, Aunt Clara thinks she
could contribute more to society if she were a cow.

#95 **"The Trial and Error of Aunt Clara"**   2/2/67
The Witches Council forces Aunt Clara to stand trial for
her bumbling ways. Samantha acts as her defense attor-
ney.

#96 **"Three Wishes"**   2/9/67
Endora grants Darrin three wishes without his knowledge, hoping she'll prove that he's having an affair.

#97   **"I Remember You ... Sometimes"**   2/16/67
Darrin thinks his instant memory book is the reason for his total recall, but it's actually the result of a spell Endora cast over his watch.

#98   **"Art for Sam's Sake"**   2/23/67
At a charity art auction, Samantha wins first prize, but only after Endora switches her still life for a masterpiece.

#99   **"Charlie Harper, Winner"**   3/2/67
Samantha uses witchcraft to teach the wife of an old friend of Darrin's a lesson on the meaning of values.

#100   **"Aunt Clara's Victoria Victory"**   3/9/67
Aunt Clara accidentally summons Queen Victoria whose morals best belong in the nineteenth century.

#101   **"The Crone of Cawdor"**   3/16/67
Darrin will turn 500 years old if he's kissed by an old crone in the body of a 24-year-old beauty.

#102   **"No More Mr. Nice Guy"**   3/23/67
Endora's spell has Darrin offending every new acquaintance that comes into his life.

#103   **"It's Wishcraft"**   3/30/67
Tabatha's been experimenting with her powers during a visit from her mortal grandparents.

#104   **"How to Fail in Business with All Kinds of Help"**
4/6/67
Darrin is determined to win the Madame Maruska cosmetic account without any help from Endora or Samantha.

#105   **"Bewitched, Bothered, and Infuriated"**   4/13/67
Darrin and Samantha try to prevent Larry from having an accident after a newspaper, conjured up by Aunt Clara, suggests he is going to break his leg.

#106 **"Nobody but a Frog Knows How to Live"**   4/27/67
A frog that has been turned into a man pesters Samantha to return him to his original form so he can be with the love of his life.

#107 **"There's Gold in Them There Pills"**   5/4/67
Larry plans to market the pills that cured Darrin's cold, unaware that they were supplied by a warlock.

The Fourth Season, 1967–68

#108 **"Long Live the Queen"**   9/7/67
Samantha is crowned Queen of the Witches. Darrin is aghast as a blackbird, walking chair, animals, supernatural things, etc., invade the house.

#109 **"Toys in Babeland"**   9/14/67
Endora teaches Tabatha how to bring her toys to life when she makes a baby-sitter out of a toy soldier.

#110 **"Business, Italian Style"**   9/21/67
Darrin tries to learn Italian to land a new account, but after some help from Endora, he has to relearn English.

#111 **"Double, Double, Toil and Trouble"**   9/28/67
While Samantha's away, Endora summons Serena to pose as her cousin and drive Darrin out of the house.

#112 **"Cheap, Cheap"**   10/5/67
Darrin is pinching pennies after Endora's spell brands him a cheapskate.

#113 **"No Zip in My Zap"**   10/12/67
Samantha loses her powers and Dr. Bombay prescribes self-levitation as the cure.

#114 **"Birdies, Bogeys, and Baxter"**   10/19/67
Samantha gives Darrin's golf game a magical boost to let the wind out of an obnoxious client who claims to be the world's greatest golfer.

#115 "The Safe and Sane Halloween"   10/26/67
Tabatha wreaks havoc on Halloween when she conjures up out of her storybook three unearthly creatures who terrorize the neighborhood.

#116 "Out of Synch, Out of Mind"   11/2/67
Darrin's mother bears witness to Aunt Clara's latest goof: Samantha's voice gets out of synch when the bumbling witch tries to synchronize a sound track to a home movie.

#117 "That Was No Chick, That Was My Wife"   11/9/67
When Samantha pops home during a business trip to Chicago, the client becomes convinced that the woman Darrin is with is not Mrs. Stephens.

#118 "Allergic to Macedonian Dodo Birds"   11/16/67
An allergy strips Endora of her powers and transfers them to Aunt Clara.

#119 "Samantha's Thanksgiving to Remember"
11/23/67
The Stephens family (and neighbor Gladys) spend Thanksgiving with the Pilgrims as Aunt Clara's misguided magic whisks them back to seventeenth century Plymouth.

#120 "Solid Gold Mother-in-Law"   11/30/67
Endora tries to make peace with Darrin by becoming a charming mother-in-law in front of an old-fashioned client.

#121 "My, What Big Ears You Have"   12/7/67
Darrin's ears grow with every little lie, thanks to a spell by Endora.

#122 "I Get Your Nanny, You Get My Goat"   12/14/67
Darrin is pleased with the new nanny, Elspeth, but Elspeth's former employer, Lord Montdrako, wants her back and nothing will stop him from getting her.

#123 **"Humbug Not to Be Spoken Here"**   **12/21/67**
Samantha tries to inspire a Scrooge-like client with some Christmas cheer.

#124 **"Samantha's da Vinci Dilemma"**   **12/28/67**
Samantha needs somebody to paint the house, so Aunt Clara summons Leonardo da Vinci.

#125 **"Once in a Vial"**   **1/4/68**
Endora's plan for an ex-beau of Samantha's to reclaim her backfires when a love potion meant for Samantha winds up in Endora's drink.

#126 **"Snob in the Grass"**   **1/11/68**
The Stephens pay a return visit to Sheila Sommers. Sheila tries to restake her claim on Darrin until Samantha gives her a well-deserved twitch.

#127 **"If They Never Met"**   **1/25/68**
Endora sends Darrin back to a time and place where he would be if he had never met Samantha.

#128 **"Hippie, Hippie, Hooray"**   **2/1/68**
Samantha gets the glory when her look-alike cousin, Serena, is arrested during a peace riot.

#129 **"A Prince of a Guy"**   **2/8/68**
Tabatha zaps Prince Charming out of her "Sleeping Beauty" storybook and the mortal women who meet him are taken in by his superficial charms.

#130 **"McTavish"**   **2/15/68**
The Stephens' home is haunted when a ghost takes up residence after Samantha convinces him to leave an old English castle.

#131 **"How Green Was My Grass"**   **2/29/68**
The Stephens receive a lawn of artificial grass by mistake, but Darrin thinks Samantha conjured it up.

#132 **"To Twitch or Not to Twitch"**   **3/14/68**

A flat tire in the rain sparks a heated argument between Darrin and Samantha over when it's acceptable for her to use her powers.

#133 **"Playmates"**   **3/21/68**

Tabitha solves a bully problem by changing a pesky playmate into a bulldog.

#134 **"Tabitha's Cranky Spell"**   **3/28/68**

Tabitha's witchcraft has her baby-sitter convinced that she has contacted the spirit world.

#135 **"I Confess"**   **4/4/68**

Samantha's spell has Darrin dreaming of what life would be like if she confessed her witchly ways to the world.

#136 **"A Majority of Two"**   **4/11/68**

Rebounding from a broken romance, Aunt Clara gets involved with a Japanese widower, a client of McMann and Tate.

#137 **"Samantha's Secret Saucer"**   **4/18/68**

The Stephens play host to a pair of space aliens after Aunt Clara places a flying saucer in the back yard.

#138 **"The No-Harm Charm"**   **4/25/68**

Uncle Arthur tries to boost Darrin's confidence by giving him a so-called lucky charm to protect him from all evil.

#139 **"Man of the Year"**   **5/2/68**

Darrin wins an advertising award and the publicity goes to his head when Endora casts a spell that has him believing his own press.

#140 **"Splitsville"**   **5/16/68**

Gladys wears out her welcome at the Stephens' house when she moves in after a fight with Abner.

The Fifth Season, 1968–69

#141 **"Samantha's Wedding Present"** 9/26/68
Darrin is feeling small after Endora's spell shrinks him down to size.

#142 **"Samantha Goes South for a Spell"** 10/3/68
Darrin must rescue Samantha who's been sent to 1868 New Orleans by a jealous witch.

#143 **"Samantha on the Keyboard"** 10/10/68
Samantha takes piano lessons to prove to Tabitha and Endora that it can be done the mortal way.

#144 **"Darrin Gone and Forgotten"** 10/17/68
Darrin is sent away by Carlotta, a powerful witch who insists that Samantha marry her son, Juke.

#145 **"It's So Nice to Have a Spouse Around the House"** 10/24/68
While Samantha is off at a meeting of the Witches Council, Darrin mistakenly takes her look-alike cousin, Serena, on a second honeymoon.

#146 **"Mirror, Mirror on the Wall"** 11/7/68
Darrin has a love affair with himself after Endora casts a spell on him to prove that mortals are vain creatures.

#147 **"Samantha's French Pastry"** 11/14/68
The Emperor Napoleon pays the Stephens a visit when Uncle Arthur tries to conjure up a French dessert.

#148 **"Is It Magic or Imagination?"** 11/21/68
Larry offers Samantha a job at McMann and Tate after she wins a trip to Tahiti in a slogan contest.

#149 **"Samantha Fights City Hall"** 11/28/68
Civic affairs get a boost from the supernatural when Samantha fights to save a neighborhood park.

#150 "Samantha Loses Her Voice"   12/5/68
Uncle Arthur's spell has Samantha speaking in Darrin's voice and vice versa. Meanwhile, the Stephens are trying to settle an argument between the Tates.

#151 "I Don't Want to be a Toad"   12/12/68
On her first (and last) day in nursery school, Tabitha grants a classmate's request by changing her into a butterfly.

#152 "Weep No More, My Willow"   12/19/68
Dr. Bombay branches out by curing a weeping willow, but Samantha gets caught in the fallout and can't stop weeping.

#153 "Instant Courtesy"   12/26/68
Convinced her son-in-law is rude and inconsiderate, Endora zaps Darrin with a dose of gallantry.

#154 "Samantha's Super Maid"   1/2/69
Samantha tries to get rid of the new maid Phyllis insisted she hire before the maid discovers any witchly occurrences.

#155 "Serena Strikes Again," Part 1   1/9/69
In an attempt to protect her cousin, Serena changes an amorous client in hot pursuit of Darrin into a monkey.

#156 "Serena Strikes Again," Part 2   1/16/69
Darrin pleads with Serena to change his client back into a woman, but the monkey has escaped and ends up in the hands of an organ grinder.

#157 "One Touch of Midas"   1/23/69
Darrin's hopes for successfully marketing a new "Fuzz Doll" are deflated when he learns that Endora is responsible for its instant popularity.

#158 **"Samantha, the Bard"**   **1/30/69**
Samantha's ill . . .
It's her speech this time.
All of her words
Tumble out in rhyme.

#159 **"Samantha, the Sculptress"**   **2/6/69**
Endora makes busts of Darrin and Larry. The talking clay heads of their likenesses bewilder a prospective client.

#160 **"Mrs. Stephens, Where Are You?"**   **2/13/69**
Serena turns Darrin's mother into a cat after finding her remarks about Samantha's family insulting.

#161 **"Marriage, Witches' Style"**   **2/20/69**
Tired of the warlock scene, Serena turns to a computer dating service to find a mortal husband.

#162 **"Going Ape"**   **2/27/69**
Samantha turns a stray chimp into a man who ends up in a TV commercial for men's cologne.

#163 **"Tabitha's Weekend"**   **3/6/69**
Samantha accompanies Tabitha on a weekend visit with her mortal grandparents, hoping to prevent her from spilling the fact that mother and daughter are witches.

#164 **"The Battle of Burning Oak"**   **3/13/69**
Endora turns Darrin into a snob as he and Samantha are being considered for membership at an exclusive country club.

#165 **"Samantha's Power Failure"**   **3/20/69**
The Witches Council strips Samantha of her powers for refusing to give up Darrin. Uncle Arthur and Serena support Samantha, find themselves without their powers, and are forced to get jobs in an ice cream factory.

#166   "Samantha Twitches for UNICEF"   **3/27/69**
Samantha pulls out all the stops to reclaim $10,000 from a man who welshed on a UNICEF pledge.

#167   "Daddy Does His Thing"   **4/3/69**
Maurice turns Darrin into a mule for refusing to accept his generous birthday gift.

#168   "Samantha's Good News"   **4/10/69**
Samantha tries to save her parents 2,000-year-old marriage and later reveals that she is going to have another baby.

#169   "Samantha's Shopping Spree"   **4/17/69**
Cousin Henry causes chaos in a department store when he changes an overzealous salesman into a mannequin.

#170   "Samantha and Darrin in Mexico City"   **4/24/69**
Darrin has to make a speech in Spanish, but, thanks to Endora, he disappears every time he speaks a word of it.

The Sixth Season, 1969–70

#171   "Samantha and the Beanstalk"   **9/18/69**
Tabitha visits the storybook world of "Jack and the Beanstalk" after deciding that her parents prefer boys to girls.

#172   "Samantha's Yoo-Hoo Maid"   **9/25/69**
The Stephens' new maid, Esmeralda, is a shy witch who fades out when she's nervous and conjures things up when she sneezes.

#173   "Samantha's Caesar Salad"   **10/2/69**
Julius Caesar pays a visit to the twentieth century after bumbling Esmeralda conjures up the Emperor instead of the famous salad.

#174 **"Samantha's Curious Cravings"** **10/9/69**
Pregnant Samantha's food cravings are conveniently satisfied since every time she has a yen for something to eat, it magically appears.

#175 **"And Something Makes Four"** **10/16/69**
Samantha gives birth to a boy and thanks to Maurice's spell, the whole world falls in love with the new arrival.

#176 **"Naming Samantha's New Baby"** **10/23/69**
Maurice is disappointed to learn that the new baby was not named after him.

#177 **"To Trick or Treat or Not to Trick or Treat"**
10/30/69
On Halloween, Endora transforms Darrin into the stereotypical witch he depicted her to be, and will not change him back unless Samantha promises *not* to go trick-or-treating with Tabitha.

#178 **"A Bunny for Tabitha"** **11/6/69**
Uncle Arthur accidentally changes the rabbit Tabitha wished for as a birthday present into a Playboy Bunny and is having trouble reversing the spell.

#179 **"Samantha's Secret Spell"** **11/13/69**
Endora plans to turn Darrin into a mouse at midnight unless Samantha can come up with a counterspell.

#180 **"Daddy Comes for a Visit"** **11/20/69**
Against his better judgment, Darrin accepts a watch from Maurice that enables him to perform witchcraft.

#181 **"Darrin, the Warlock"** **11/27/69**
With Darrin's powers going to his head, Samantha worries that her husband is no longer the man she married.

#182 "Samantha's Double Mother Trouble"   12/4/69
Darrin's mother takes refuge at the Stephens' after a fight with her husband. Meanwhile, Esmeralda mistakenly conjures up Mother Goose out of her book of rhymes.

#183 "You're So Agreeable"   12/11/69
Endora's spell has Darrin saying "yes" to everyone, including Larry, who shows him the door after blowing it with a client.

**#184 "Santa Comes to Visit and Stays and Stays"
12/18/69**
Santa Claus is stuck at the Stephens' house when Esmeralda accidentally materializes him the night before Christmas.

#185 "Samantha's Better Halves"   1/1/70
Flashbacks recall the time Endora split Darrin in two so he could attend an important business meeting in Japan *and* tend to his pregnant wife.

#186 "Samantha's Lost Weekend"   1/8/70
Samantha goes on an eating binge after she drinks from a hexed glass of milk Esmeralda had intended for Tabitha.

#187 "The Phrase Is Familiar"   1/15/70
Endora casts a spell that has Darrin talking in cliches.

#188 "Samantha's Secret Is Discovered"   1/22/70
After being caught in the act, Samantha confesses her witchly ways to Mrs. Stephens, but when the Witches Council revokes Sam's powers, she must find another way to convince her mother-in-law that she has not lost her mind.

#189 "Tabitha's Very Own Samantha"   1/29/70
Feeling neglected by the attention given to her new baby brother, Tabitha conjures up a duplicate Samantha, a mother she does not have to share with anyone.

#190 "Super Arthur" 2/5/70
Uncle Arthur's powers have gone haywire, with strange occurrences happening to him while he awaits a cure from Dr. Bombay.

#191 "What Makes Darrin Run" 2/12/70
Endora transforms a less than ambitious Darrin into a power-driven maniac.

#192 "Serena Stops the Show" 2/19/70
Entertainment chairman, Serena, wants the musical duo of Boyce and Hart to appear at the Cosmos Cotillion.

#193 "Just a Kid Again" 2/26/70
A toy-store salesman gets more than he bargained for when he confesses to Tabitha his wish to be nine years old again.

#194 "The Generation Zap" 3/5/70
A client's daughter falls in love with Darrin, thanks to some witchly interference from Endora and Serena.

#195 "Okay, Who's the Wise Witch?" 3/12/70
The Stephens' home is sealed off by witchcraft, the result of a vapor lock caused by Samantha's non-use of her powers.

#196 "A Chance on Love" 3/19/70
While posing as Samantha in a hotel lobby, Serena meets and has a fling with a client of McMann and Tate.

#197 "If the Shoe Pinches" 3/26/70
Endora summons a nasty leprechaun to stir up trouble for Darrin.

#198 "Mona, Sammy" 4/2/70
Darrin is credited as the artist when Samantha's face appears on a Mona Lisa–type portrait. An envious Louise wants Darrin to paint a portrait of her, as well.

#199   "Turn on the Old Charm"   4/9/70
   Samantha gives Darrin a magic amulet that transforms Endora into a loving mother-in-law.

#200   "Make Love, Not Hate"   4/16/70
   Chaos erupts at the Stephens' during a dinner party, when a love potion meant to get a man for Esmeralda ends up in the clam dip.

The Seventh Season, 1970–71

#201   "To Go or Not To Go, That Is the Question," Part 1 9/24/70
   Samantha has been ordered by the High Priestess Hepzibah to attend a Witches Convention in Salem, Massachusetts, and Darrin is not invited!

#202   "Salem, Here We Come," Part 2   10/1/70
   Hepzibah resides in the Stephens' home to determine whether or not the mixed marriage should be dissolved.

#203   "The Salem Saga," Part 1   10/8/70
   On a tour of the House of Seven Gables, Samantha encounters trouble with a warlock who's been turned into an antique bed warmer.

#204   "Samantha's Hot Bed Warmer," Part 2   10/15/70
   While Darrin remains in jail, accused of stealing the bed warmer, Samantha searches for the spell to change it back to its original form.

#205   "Darrin on a Pedestal"   10/22/70
   In Gloucester, Massachusetts, Darrin tries to keep a stiff upper lip after Serena zaps the famed Fisherman's Memorial to life and replaces the statue with him.

#206   "Paul Revere Rides Again"   10/29/70
   Paul Revere pays an unexpected visit to the twentieth century when Esmeralda tries to send a Colonial teapot back to Samantha.

#207 **"Samantha's Bad Day in Salem"**   11/5/70
  Trouble and confusion run rampant when a lovesick warlock conjures up his own Samantha when he realizes he cannot have the real one.

#208 **"Samantha's Old Salem Trip"**   11/12/70
  Endora sends Darrin back in time to rescue Samantha, who's been accidentally zapped to seventeenth century Salem by Esmeralda.

#209 **"Samantha's Pet Warlock"**   11/19/70
  An old suitor tries to win his way back into Samantha's life disguised as a stray mutt.

#210 **"Samantha's Old Man"**   12/3/70
  The future becomes the present when Endora changes Darrin into a 72-year-old man.

#211 **"The Corsican Cousins"**   12/10/70
  Endora would like Samantha to be more like Serena, so she casts a spell that has the two cousins sharing personalities.

#212 **"Samantha's Magic Potion"**   12/17/70
  Samantha tries to convince Darrin that the run of bad luck he's been having at work is not due to witchcraft.

#213 **"Sisters at Heart"**   12/24/70
  It's a White Christmas . . . *and* a Black one when Tabitha and her friend, Lisa, teach a bigoted client a lesson in racism.

#214 **"Mother-in-law of the Year"**   1/14/71
  Endora agrees to appear on a TV commercial for Darrin's client, but backs out at the last minute.

#215 **"Mary, the Good Fairy," Part 1**   1/21/71
  Samantha subs for the Good Fairy who's determined to trade in her wings for domestic life.

#216　"The Good Fairy Strikes Again," Part 2　　1/28/71
Mary is enjoying an early retirement while Samantha has unwillingly become her permanent replacement.

#217　"Return of Darrin, the Bold"　　2/4/71
Serena pays a visit to a fourteenth-century ancestor of Darrin's as part of Endora's scheme to change her son-in-law into a Warlock.

#218　"The House That Uncle Arthur Built"　　2/11/71
Uncle Arthur's engaged to be married, but only if he can leave behind his practical joking ways.

#219　"Samantha and the Troll"　　2/18/71
While standing in for Samantha who's off having a checkup, Serena charms a hair tonic client, much to the dismay of his jealous wife.

#220　"This Little Piggie"　　2/25/71
Endora turns Darrin's head into a pig's head to prove his stubbornness, but does not expect that her trickery, instead, lands him a spare ribs account.

#221　"Mixed Doubles"　　3/4/71
A restless night and a troubling dream causes Samantha to trade lives with Louise in the eyes of all mortals who know them—especially Darrin and Larry.

#222　"Darrin Goes Ape"　　3/11/71
Darrin's in the monkey cage after Serena changes him into a gorilla.

#223　"Money Happy Returns"　　3/18/71
Darrin thinks the money he found in the back seat of a cab was zapped for him by Endora.

#224　"Out of the Mouths of Babes"　　3/25/71
Darrin's a child again, thanks to Endora's magic. He uses his youthful disguise to convince a client that a slow-

selling Irish stew product had best go to the dogs. It's becomes a best-selling dog food.

#225 **"Sam's Psychic Slip"** **4/1/71**
Samantha's powers are out of control when she hiccups, the result of accepting a gift from Darrin she feels she does not deserve.

#226 **"Samantha's Magic Mirror"** **4/8/71**
Samantha tries to boost Esmeralda's confidence in time for a reunion with an old beau.

#227 **"Laugh, Clown, Laugh"** **4/15/71**
Nobody's laughing when Endora provides Darrin with an overly offensive sense of humor.

#228 **"Samantha and the Antique Doll"** **4/22/71**
Phyllis is convinced she has magical powers after she sees her grandmother's doll float across the room.

The Eighth Season, 1971–72

#229 **"How Not to Lose Your Head to King Henry VIII,"**
Part 1 **9/15/71**
Samantha becomes the prospective wife to Henry VIII when a hateful witch sends her back to sixteenth-century England.

#230 **"How Not to Lose Your Head to King Henry VIII,"**
Part 2 **9/22/71**
Endora sends Darrin back in time to rescue Samantha from Henry VIII, who plans to add her to his gallery of late wives.

#231 **"Samantha and the Loch Ness Monster"** **9/29/71**
In Scotland, Samantha persuades Serena to change the Loch Ness monster back into the warlock Serena rejected 40 years ago.

#232   **"Samantha's Not-So-Leaning Tower of Pisa"**
10/6/71
Esmeralda tries to reverse her old mistake by straightening the Leaning Tower of Pisa that she originally made lean so long ago.

#233   **"Bewitched, Bothered, and Baldoni"**   **10/13/71**
The *Statue of Venus* comes to life as part of Endora's scheme to test Darrin's fidelity.

#234   **"Paris, Witches Style"**   **10/20/71**
Maurice flies into a warlock's rage when Samantha and Darrin fail to visit him on their European tour.

#235   **"The Ghost Who Made a Specter of Himself"**
10/27/71
The Stephens and the Tates spend a harrowing weekend in an old English castle, where a lovesick ghost takes over Darrin's body to be near Samantha and flirts with Louise.

#236   **"TV or Not TV"**   **11/3/71**
Tabitha rises to stardom when she magically appears on a puppet show produced by Darrin's client.

#237   **"A Plague on Maurice and Samantha"**   **11/10/71**
Maurice samples mortal life after he loses his powers from a virus he caught from Samantha.

#238   **"Hansel and Gretel in Samanthaland"**   **11/17/71**
Hansel and Gretel come to dinner when Tabitha zaps them out of their classic storybook.

#239   **"The Warlock in the Gray Flannel Suit"**   **12/1/71**
Endora enlists the help of a hippie Warlock named Alonza to eliminate Darrin's job so that he may attend a family wedding with Samantha.

#240   **"The Eight-Year Witch"**   **12/8/71**
Endora changes a cat into a seductress, hoping to prove that Darrin has a wandering eye.

#241 **"Three Men and a Witch on a Horse"** **12/15/71**
Darrin's off to the race track after Endora's spell gives him the gambling bug.

#242 **"Adam, Warlock or Washout"** **12/29/71**
Adam's powers are being tested, but not before he receives some advanced coaching from Maurice.

#243 **"Samantha's Magic Sitter"** **1/5/72**
Esmeralda is a hit when she volunteers to baby-sit for the son of Darrin's client, but strikes out with the parents when the boy claims he was entertained by witchcraft.

#244 **"Samantha Is Earthbound"** **1/15/72**
Samantha is having trouble keeping her feet on the ground after Dr. Bombay overcures her from a strong gravitational pull.

#245 **"Serena's Richcraft"** **1/22/72**
After losing her powers, Serena resides with Sam and Darrin, where she meets and falls in love with a wealthy and attractive client.

#246 **"Samantha on Thin Ice"** **1/29/72**
Samantha and Tabitha are taking ice-skating lessons despite Endora's wishes that they do it the easy (witchly) way.

#247 **"Serena's Youth Pill"** **2/5/72**
Serena gives Larry a Vitamin V pill (for va-va-voom) that transforms today's Silver Fox into the Red Devil he was in yesteryear.

#248 **"Tabitha's First Day at School"** **2/12/72**
Samantha reluctantly enrolls Tabitha in school where, on her first day, she changes the class bully into a bullfrog and cannot reverse the spell.

#249 **"George Washington Zapped Here," Part 1** **2/19/72**
Esmeralda accidentally conjures up George Washington for Tabitha's "show and tell" school project.

#250 **"George Washington Zapped Here," Part 2**   **2/26/72**
George Washington's visit to the twentieth century concludes with his trial for threatening a police officer and speaking publicly about the Constitution.

#251 **"School Days, School Daze"**   **3/4/72**
With Endora's help, Tabitha scores high marks on a second-grade entrance exam.

#252 **"A Good Turn Never Goes Unpunished"**   **3/11/72**
Darrin suspects that Samantha's brilliant ideas for Benson's Sleep EZ Mattresses are the product of witchcraft.

#253 **"Sam's Witchcraft Blows a Fuse"**   **3/18/72**
Samantha is suffering from a loss of power and a red-checkered face, while Darrin is in hot pursuit of a dodo bird's tail feather needed for the cure.

#254 **"The Truth, Nothing but the Truth, So Help Me Sam"**
3/25/72
A dinner party ends in disaster when a truth spell cast by Endora causes everyone to say what is on their minds.

THE
Bewitched
FAN CLUB

For information regarding personal appearances or the activities of:

Kasey Rogers (Louise Tate)
Bernard Fox (Dr. Bombay)
Sandra Gould (Gladys Kravitz)
Alice Ghostley (Esmeralda)
Mark Wood (*Bewitched* authority and co-author)
Scott Awley (artist)

PLEASE CONTACT:

The Bartels Company
Kathy Bartels
Post Office Box 57593
Sherman Oaks, CA 91403

TEL: (818) 505-9084   **FAX: (818) 761-0267**
PAGER: (818) 513-2418   **CELL: (818) 970-8404**

ACKNOWLEDGMENTS

Our very special thanks for support, sweat, contributions, and love to:

Barry Perelman	Where it all started
Bill Birnes	Who made it all possible
Sony Signature	Cathy Bitran, Jack Westercamp, and all the others at Sony who helped clear the boards
Kensington Publishing Kate Duffy	Our wonderful editor with that incredible sense of humor (And, boy, did she need it!)
Beth Leiberman	Who had faith in the first place
Scott Awley	For his wonderful Art. Scott did the original re-created front and back cover cels
Steven Colbert	For infinite patience, research, Episode Outlines, loans of tapes and pictures, etc., etc.
Steve Cox	Thanks for the photos, Steve.
Herbie J. Pilato	Author of *The* Bewitched *Book* and the soon-to-be-released Bewitched *Forever*, Herbie introduced Mark

and Kasey to each other about
1990. Thanks, Herbie, and thanks
for the photos, too.

More thanks to family and friends for digging up old family favorites:

Kate W. Alvarado, Delbert Bybee, Annette Bouyer, Annie and Jay Donnellan, Dr. and Mrs. Douglas Dick, Jacqueline and Bernard Fox, Wanda Gira, Candace J. Hallock, Howard and Averil Koch, Larry and Pauline Kuhns, Mike and DeeDee Lewis, Monika Lewis, Jules Monroe, Gina Park, Angie and Jim Rogers, Pepper Shoaff, Mona and Jim Strauss with Vinita and Varsha, Patricia H. West, Shirley and Marion Wood, and all the ladies of the Bennett Woods Garden Club of Smyrna, Georgia.

ABOUT THE AUTHORS

KASEY ROGERS

You know the face, but . . . what's her name?

From the bouncy Louise Tate of *Bewitched* to the long-suffering Julie Anderson of *Peyton Place* to the conniving Miriam of Hitchcock's *Strangers on a Train*, you've probably grown up watching Kasey on television and the silver screen and never known her name. Either one of them.

Kasey started her career under contract to Paramount Studios, where they gave her the name of Laura Elliot. During her five-year stint at the studio, she starred, or was a member of the supporting cast, in 28 films, including *Strangers on a Train, Silver City, The Denver and the Rio Grande, Jamaica Run, Two Lost Worlds,* etc. As a young contract player she also appeared in *A Place in the Sun, Riding High, Samson and Delilah,* and others.

Upon leaving Paramount, Kasey left the "Laura Elliot" moniker behind and resumed her own name. All of her television appearances (over 600) are as Kasey Rogers.

Besides *Bewitched,* they include multiple appearances in *The Lucy Show, Perry Mason, Mission Impossible, Wanted, Dead or Alive, Maverick, Marcus Welby,* and many, many more.

The Bewitched *Cookbook* is not her first foray into the literary world. She sold her first script to Universal many years ago, was a featured columnist for the *Los Angeles Herald-Examiner* and wrote for numerous national magazines on her other favorite subject, motorcycle racing! Let's hear it for Louise Tate cooking on her Honda! What would Larry say?

MARK WOOD

Mark was bewitched by Hollywood at a young age, literally! Raised in Atlanta, Georgia, he traveled to Hollywood four years ago to make his life's dream come true: a spin-off series of *Bewitched* called *Bewitched Again.* Mark has always wanted to play Samantha and Darrin's little boy, Adam, grown up. (Yes, he *can* twitch his nose like Samantha!) It hasn't happened . . . yet!

But, he did get to meet the entire cast of *Bewitched* and make lifelong friends of them. He even moved into "Louise Tate's" spare room!

Mark has numerous credits in the fields of comedy, singing, writing, and costume designing including *Heat of the Night, I'll Fly Away, Six Flags Over Georgia,* and others.

In addition to *The* Bewitched *Cookbook,* Mark and Kasey have written a new show called (Can you stand it?) "Son Of A Witch," the story of America's first male witch, just in case the *Bewitched Again* idea doesn't *fly.*

Keep those TVs tuned.